Quick Quotes
for
Church Bulletins

Quick Quotes for Church Bulletins

by
Paul E. Holdcraft

ABINGDON
Nashville

QUICK QUOTES FOR CHURCH BULLETINS

Copyright 1955 by Pierce & Washabaugh

Eleventh Printing 1978

All rights in this book are reserved.
No part of the book may be reproduced in any manner whatsoever without written permission of the publisher except brief quotations embodied in critical articles or reviews. For information address Abingdon, Nashville, Tennessee.

ISBN 0-687-35168-5

MANUFACTURED BY THE PARTHENON PRESS AT
NASHVILLE, TENNESSEE, UNITED STATES OF AMERICA

PREFACE

An interesting, if not plausible, story is told of a preacher who always used two gestures when he preached. As he started his sermon, he held up two fingers of his right hand, and at the conclusion he held up two fingers of his left hand. When asked the meaning of these gestures, he said: "They are quotation marks." From beginning to end he was quoting sermons he had read from books. His two gestures were his dubious way of being intellectually honest.

Perhaps something like this should be done with this compilation. The contents are practically all quotations gathered from countless sources over a long period of years. In most cases the authors are not known. When known, a credit line appears.

The purpose of the compilation is to put into the hands of busy pastors and church workers, as the title clearly implies, *Quick Quotes for Church Bulletins*. In cutting stencils or preparing copy for the Sunday bulletin, after all announcements have been cared for, a few lines are available for inspirational items. Here is where this little book offers its services. Likewise, the outside bulletin board offers opportunities to preach silent sermonettes to passers-by. A pungent sentence will reach many who never enter a church. It is hoped that the contents of this book will help the church to help others.

PAUL E. HOLDCRAFT

CONTENTS

I. **Special Days and Occasions** 9

   New Year 9
   Youth Week (See Chapter IV)
   Lincoln's Birthday; Washington's Birthday (See Chapter III)
   Lent and Holy Week 11
   Palm Sunday 14
   Easter; Immortality 15
   Mother's Day; Christian Family Week 17
   Memorial Day (See Chapter III)
   Pentecost 19
   Commencement (See Chapter V)
   Children's Day (See Chapter IV)
   Independence Day (See Chapter III)
   Vacation Time 21
   Labor Day 21
   Rally Day (See Chapter II)
   Reformation Sunday 25
   Veterans' Day (See Chapter III)
   Thanksgiving 26
   Bible Sunday (See Chapter VIII)
   Advent and Christmas 28

II. **Church Attendance — The Sabbath — Christian Worship and Work** 31

III. **Patriotism—Citizenship—War and Peace** 41

IV. **Children and Youth** 47

V. **Christian Education** 49

VI.	The Stewardship of Money	53
VII.	Missions and Evangelism	57
VIII.	The Holy Bible	60
IX.	Temperance	63
X.	Religious Life and Action	67

Chapter I

Special Days and Occasions

NEW YEAR

New Year's Day—a milepost on the way to eternity.

Have nothing to do with that which will not bear the test of time.

Time, whose tooth gnaws away everything, is powerless against truth.
—Thomas Huxley

Taking the long view—backward and forward—it is impossible for a Christian to be a defeatist. The right wins finally.

Time is but the fringe of eternity.

Our lives are judged not so much by their length of days and years as by their breadth of visions and sympathies and outlook.
—*Western Recorder*

The New Year offers the old world a new chance.

A day is a wonderful thing. It is like a great doorway flung wide for you to pass through into all manner of adventures.   —St. Nicholas

Full usefulness depends on new thoughts and new horizons. Life must look to the future, not to the past.

Take time to live—it is the secret of success.
Take time to think—it is the source of power.
Take time to play—it is the secret of youth.
Take time to read—it is the foundation of knowledge.
Take time for friendship—it is the source of happiness.
Take time to laugh—it helps lift life's load.
Take time to dream—it hitches the soul to the stars.
Take time for God—it is life's only lasting investment.
—*Rotary Rambler*, Norton, Kansas

No longer forward or behind
I look in hope or fear;
But, grateful, take the good I find,
The best of now and here.
—John Greenleaf Whittier

God's mercies are as old as eternity and yet they are new every morning.

Be patient enough to live one day at a time as Jesus taught us, letting yesterday go, and leaving tomorrow till it arrives.—Joseph Fort Newton

Well arranged time is the surest mark of a well arranged mind.
—Sir Isaac Pitman

We always have time enough if we use it aright.   —Goethe

Go as far as you can see, and when you get there you will see farther.
—Elbert Hubbard

One of our troubles is that we let resolutions take the place of resolution.

I shall pass through this world but once. Any good, therefore, that I can do, or any kindness that I can show, let me do it now; let me not defer or neglect it, for I shall not pass this way again.   —Author Unknown

Life is a voyage; the human soul a ship. The uncharted seas of the New Year lie before us. It will not be all calm seas and sunny skies. There will also be shoals and reefs and storms. What a comfort it is, when the shoals of temptation threaten, the reefs of trouble rise, and the storms of sorrow surround us, to know that Jesus is the Captain of our souls and His Word the chart of our voyage. —W. F. Wilk

As I enter the New Year, I take God to be my Father; Jesus Christ to be my Saviour; the Holy Spirit to be my Guide; the Bible to be the rule of my life; Christian people to be my associates; Christian work my duty and privilege.

Translate your resolutions into definite deeds or else you will forget them.

In the New Year your every thought, word, and deed will be recorded. God's bookkeeper makes no mistakes.

The best forethought for tomorrow is today's duty well done.

Have courage to let go the things not worth sticking to.

In the New Year take time to be holy. Let the world rush on.

We need an unchanging Christ for the changing years. Jesus Christ is "the same yesterday, today, and forever."

There is something you can do to make this world better. You can contribute one consecrated life.

I know not the way He leads me, but well do I know my Guide. What have I to fear? —Martin Luther

Live your best, and act your best, and think your best each day, for there may be no tomorrows.

You can't change the past, but you can ruin a perfectly good present by worrying about the future.

Some people have yet to learn that they cannot travel in the wrong direction and reach the right destination.

Whatever your past has been, you have a spotless future.

Life is measured by its depth, not its duration.

The right use of today is the best preparation for tomorrow.

The great use of life is to spend it for something that outlasts it.
—William James

I would rather walk with God in the dark than go alone in the light.
—Mary Gardiner Brainard

For my part, I live every day as though it were the first day I had ever seen and the last I were going to see. —William Lyon Phelps

Good resolutions carried out become good habits.

If time be of all things most precious, then wasting time is the greatest prodigality; for lost time is never found again. —Benjamin Franklin

There never was a time like now to square yourself with God.

The man who does not learn by his mistakes turns his best schoolmaster out of doors.

Daily devotions help you meet the problems of life one day at a time.

A good memory test is to sit down and try to recall the things you worried about at this time last year.

Like Enoch, walk with God this New Year. But remember that to walk with God, you must walk in the direction in which God goes.

Your life is rapidly running its course. It will be a misspent life if you reach the end of the road without the companionship of Christ.

New Year's Day is a turning point between the failures and faults of the past and the better and braver deeds of the future.

Today is the second chance which God gives us to right the wrongs, correct the mistakes, and readjust the differences that marred our yesterdays. Today is another opportunity to cancel, to expiate, to raise, to adorn.

The mill will never grind with the water that is past.—Sarah Dowdey

Making the most of today is the best way to be ready for tomorrow.

Past failures are guideposts for future success.

It's not how long but how well we live that matters.

Let me but live my life from year to year with forward face and unreluctant soul.   —Henry van Dyke

The New Year offers you fifty-two special Sabbath Day appointments with God. Will you keep them?

> The world is wide
> In time and tide,
> And—God is guide;
> Then do not hurry.
>
> That man is blest
> Who does his best
> And leaves the rest;
> Then do not worry.
> —Charles F. Deems

We live in deeds, not years; in
  thoughts, not breaths;
In feelings, not in figures on a dial.
We should count time by heart-throbs.
  He most lives
Who thinks most, feels the noblest,
  acts the best.
—Philip James Bailey

Dost thou love life? Then do not squander time, for that is the stuff life is made of.   —Benjamin Franklin

Counting time is not nearly as important as making time count.

No one can walk backward into the future.

These are the good old days we will be longing for a few years from now.
—John J. Sutter

Today is the tomorrow you worried about yesterday.

Lost time is never found.

It is later than you think.—Inscription on a sundial in an Old World cathedral yard

I am resolved
—To live with all my might while I do live;
—Never to lose one moment of time, but improve it in the most profitable way I possibly can;
—Never to do anything which I should despise or think meanly of in another;
—Never to do anything out of revenge;
—Never to do anything which I should be afraid to do if it were the last hour of my life.
—Jonathan Edwards

A New Year's Prayer
Keep thou my feet: I do not ask to see
The distant scene; one step enough
  for me.
—John Henry Newman

LENT AND HOLY WEEK

The world never needed Lent as it needs it now. Life is so strenuous and our pace so rapid. "The world is too much with us." We are so apt to forget that we have immortal spirits. Lent teaches us to be still and sense the presence of God, and listen to the still, small voice. An observance of this blessed season cannot but make us better, stronger, purer, and saner, as it prepares us for the life that shall endless be.

Do not let the trivialities of life blind you to the supreme importance of things eternal.

Attend the Passiontide services and get acquainted, or renew acquaintance, with Him who alone is "the way, the truth, and the life," and without whom "no man cometh unto the Father."

The Lenten season is not a call to exotic devotion, but a call back to normal religious living. It is because we have not been living as we should that we need these periods of concentration on spiritual values.

In the holy quiet of this hour, let us draw nigh unto Him who heareth prayer; and let us remember that he listeneth more to our hearts than to our words.

The Lenten season calls for a consecration of both life and possessions to Christ and His glorious Church. The measure of blessing we received from an observance of Lent will depend upon our response to its appeal.

Prayer is the connecting link between this life and that which is soon to be.

Prayers from the lowest depths ascend the highest.

Religion is neither a *winter* resort nor a *last* resort.

Any man who is too busy to pray is busier than God ever intended he should be. —*Baptist Recorder*

The doctrine of the cross is not a formula for the mind, but a principle of life.

Thou hast made us for Thyself, and restless are our hearts until they shall have found rest in Thee.—Augustine

You deny Christ when you fail to deny yourself for Christ.

Your religion will do more for you if you do more for it.

Take it from me, the Church has something you need more than you need anything else.

Shall I grudge to spend my life for Him who did not grudge to shed His life-blood for me? —Beveridge

Three men died on Calvary: one *for* sin, one *in* sin, and one *to* sin. These three propositions cover the whole human race. Do not die *in* sin. Die *to* it by receiving as your Saviour Him who died *for* it in your stead.
—George Guille

Jesus proved that a sinless life can be lived in a sinful world.

The religion of Jesus needs examples more than advocates.

Someone must be supreme in our lives. If it is not Jesus Christ, it will be someone else—and less—than He.

An overfed body may conceal an underfed soul.

Be content with what you have, but never with what you are.
—W. B. Millard

Again and again I have been tempted to give up the struggle, but always the figure of that strange man hanging upon the cross sends me back to my task again. —George Tyrrell

Wearing a cross cannot take the place of bearing a cross.

Difficulties strengthen the mind as labor does the body. —Seneca

A halfhearted Christian is just half a Christian.

There is no short cut to the heavenly Kingdom. It is not the way across, but the way of the Cross, that leads home.

The cross was intended as a thing of degradation, but Jesus made it a thing of dignity.

If bitterness has crept into the heart in the friction of the busy day's unguarded moments, be sure it steals away with the setting sun. Twilight is God's interval for peacemaking.

All that was taught by the Passover is realized in the Lord's Supper and the death which it commemorates. Deliverance from bondage, safety behind the sprinkled blood, fellowship around the life-giver—all these the simple feast sets forth and confirms. Jesus is the host, we are his welcomed guests, and there is never any lack of provision at His table. —*The Expositor*

The Lord's Supper is a commemoration, a communion, and a consecration. In it we remember Christ, we commune with Him and one another, and we consecrate ourselves afresh to His service.

My church represents Christ's best gift to me. I have united with it in solemn covenant that it shall have my best in attendance, prayer, service, sacrifice, zeal, giving, patience, and love. To be loyal to Christ, I must be loyal to His Church.

A Christianity without the Cross is a miserable counterfeit.

What is the matter with the church? Look in the mirror.

In the rush and noise of life, as you have intervals step home within yourselves, and be still. Wait upon God to feel His good presence; this will carry you evenly through your day's business. —William Penn

To really glory in the cross of Christ, one has to glory in his own.

The difference between "duty" and "love" is that the first represents Sinai and the second represents Calvary.

The man who walks with God always knows in what direction he is going.

Jesus, Thou Joy of loving hearts!
  Thou Fount of life! Thou Light of men!
From the best bliss that earth imparts,
  We turn unfilled to Thee again.
    —Bernard of Clairvaux

The cross is yet more conspicuous in creed than in practice.

There are still among us many Pontius Pilates who try to wash their hands of responsibility.

Drop Thy still dews of quietness,
  Till all our strivings cease;
Take from our souls the strain and stress,
And let our ordered lives confess
  The beauty of Thy peace.
    —John Greenleaf Whittier

Still as of old
Men by themselves are priced—
For thirty pieces Judas sold
Himself, not Christ.
  —Hester H. Cholmondeley

The cross bearers here will be the crown wearers "over there."

Whatsoever is bad during Lent is bad also the rest of the year.

The cross is the center of the world's history. The incarnation of Christ and the crucifixion of our Lord are the pivot round which all the events of the ages revolve.
  —Alexander Maclaren

The world is not through with the cross, but it will soon be through without it.

Christ *died* for you, and asks you to *live* for Him.

Never does human nature seem so glorious and so wicked all at once as when we stand before the cross of Jesus! The most enthusiastic hopes, the most profound humiliation, have found their inspiration there.
  —Phillips Brooks

The dark forces that incited a misguided mob to shout for the death of Christ are today just as evil, active and aggressive as they were two thousand years ago. —Igor I. Sikorsky

They gave Him a manger for a cradle, a carpenter's bench for a pulpit, thorns for a crown, and a cross for a throne. He took them and made them the very glory of His career.
  —W. E. Orchard

PALM SUNDAY

The Christian's enthusiasm should be so great as to attract attention and move the world and lead people to inquire concerning the Saviour, "Who is this?"

We need no leaping, running, branch-breaking, cloak-throwing, shouting multitudes, but men and women who day by day will follow calmly, steadily the line of the life that Christ lived.
—*Doran's Manual*

There can be no enthronement of Christ without the dethronement of self.

My kingdom is not of this world.
—Jesus

"Hosanna!" or "Crucify!"
Which is the word we cry?

I will place no value on anything I have or may possess except in relation to the Kingdom of Christ.
—David Livingstone

Lead on, O King Eternal!

A Palm Sunday prayer: Thy Kingdom come. Thy will be done in earth, as it is in heaven.

Dear to the heart of the Christian world is the story of Christ's one day of triumph. The Church rejoices because even for one brief day he was hailed on earth as King.

The triumphal procession of Christ is still going on, across continents and centuries; and it will continue, growing brighter, larger, more enthusiastic, till he enters the new Jerusalem as "King of kings and Lord of lords."

The lesson of the triumphal entry will fail of its purpose if it leaves unsaid and unwritten the fact of his glory being proclaimed today in hearts and lives made better, sweeter, by his words of power; and we proclaim him King when we offer for his use time, talents, wealth, character, and, in fact, all we have and are.

Bring forth the royal diadem,
And crown Him Lord of all!
—Edward Perronet

The man who gets a good look at Jesus Christ will never be the same man again.

Here is a king who was born in a stable, cradled in a manger, and trained in a despised village called Nazareth. He wore no imposing regalia, no royal apparel, and displayed none of the earthly trappings of royalty. His courtiers were fishermen and his throne a cross. He was without a palace, was often without food, and sometimes a fugitive. Yet today his name is the most widely known and fondly loved on earth.
—Author Unknown

I am of the opinion that we should endeavor with all possible zeal to obtain an exact understanding of the great personality of Jesus and to reclaim him for Judaism.
—M. Lazarus, Jewish Professor

I love and venerate the religion of Christ, because Christ came into the world to deliver humanity from slavery, for which God had not created it. —Giuseppe Garibaldi

I find the name of Jesus Christ written on every page of modern history.
—George Bancroft, American Historian

One year of universal and absolute Christianity would transform every people under heaven.
—M. W. Stryker

Other men have said: "If I could only live, I would establish and perpetuate a kingdom." The Christ of Galilee said: "My death shall do it."
—Herrick Johnson

The only kingdom that will prevail in this world is the Kingdom that is not of this world.

We know very little about the details of Jesus' life before He became a public character.... Jesus' life had

been so commonplace and even poor in its material circumstances that the portrayal of it would have hindered rather than helped in the presentation of Him to the Greco-Roman world as the majestic Messiah of God, the Lord of Heaven and earth.
—Edward Increase Bosworth

Jesus taught the coming of the kingdom of God, but this included also a new national morality for kingdoms of this world. He condensed the law into two sentences: "Love God" and "Love your neighbor."
—Sir Hall Caine

EASTER; IMMORTALITY

Easter verbs: "Come!" "See!" "Go!" "Tell!"

On that first Easter day life and death faced each other in mortal combat. And life won.

The risen life is the best testimony to a risen Christ.

Benjamin Franklin wrote the following epitaph for his own tomb: "The body of Benjamin Franklin, Printer, Like the Cover of an Old Book, Its Contents Torn Out and Stripped of Its Lettering and Gilding, Lies Here, Food for Worms. Yet the Work Itself shall not be Lost; for it will, as He Believed, Appear once More in a New and More Beautiful Edition, Corrected and Amended by The Author."

Our Message—A Living Christ for a Dying World.

Christ's resurrection gives us a certified Christianity, an accredited salvation.

Without Easter, neither Christmas nor Good Friday would have significance.

On Easter the Church strikes the note of praise and sings of victory. Faith overcomes the world and its sorrows, and sees the Celestial City shining beyond the river.

Those who have given Christ a place in their hearts know He has risen from the dead, because He lives in them.

The inn of a traveler on the way to Jerusalem. —Inscription on the grave of Dean Alford

The truest end of life is to know that life never ends.—William Penn

There is a continuing city for the continuing Christian.

Easter crowns with certainty man's hope of immortality.

Death is not a journeying into an unknown land; it is a voyage home. We are going not to a strange country, but to our Father's house, and among our kith and kin. —John Ruskin

We see in the risen Christ the end for which man was made, and the assurance that the end is within our reach. —B. F. Westcott

When belief moves in the direction of truth, it won't be long in reaching certainty.

Going to heaven when we die is first of all a matter of becoming something while we live.

Easter symbols are an egg or a butterfly, both being significant of wonderful changes, from death to life, from stagnation to motion, from darkness to light and color and beauty. These are what immortality means.

We prove our faith in the future by the plans we are making for the future.

Easter began a new order in an old world and made the old world new.

Easter makes a difference—the difference between life and death, light and darkness, hope and despair.

Easter joins with springtime in proclaiming life abundant and everlasting.

A church reverses God's order when it lets spiritual paralysis set in after it has observed Easter.

Men who have surrendered to the resurrected Jesus have His resurrection power.

A Moslem once boasted to a Christian: "When Moslems go to Mecca, they find there at least a coffin, but when Christians go to Jerusalem, they find only an empty grave."
"That is just the difference," replied the Christian. "Mohammed is dead; but Jesus Christ is not in the tomb. He is risen, He is alive forevermore."

The best news the world ever had came from a graveyard.

It is when our faces are turning heavenward that the sunshine lights upon them.

If seeds in the black earth can turn into such beautiful flowers, what might not the heart of man become in its long journey toward the stars?
—G. K. Chesterton

Through the message of Easter we have an endless hope instead of a hopeless end.

By the crowning miracle of the Resurrection unmistakable evidence is given to the world that the words and works of Jesus Christ are not the mere wisdom of some human sage, nor the sayings of a great philosopher, nor the dreams of an inspired poet, but the words and works of God.
—E. P. Dempsey

It takes more credulity to believe the critical case against the resurrection of Jesus than it does faith to believe the Apostles. —Sloan

We can't enter heaven before heaven enters us.

Many an Easter outfit costing a hundred dollars is matched—or unmatched—by a gift to Christ and the church of twenty-five cents.

Easter stands for life—here and hereafter.

The new Easter garb should not be criticized if it symbolizes "newness of life" within the garb.

God's plans for His children all fit into the fact of their immortality.

The prospect of living forever should bring little comfort unless we are fit to live forever.

Some folks are like Easter eggs—ornamented on the outside and hard-boiled on the inside.

Although the Master has gone to prepare a place for us, we must prepare ourselves for that place.

Jesus has taken away the loathsome aspect of the grave, and made it a covered passageway, a sort of triumphal arch through which Christians pass into the realm of light and glory just beyond.

"Now is Christ risen from the dead, and become the firstfruits of them that slept." Ring it out, Easter bells! Peal it forth, glad anthems of the church! Let the flowers tell in symbolic beauty their message that life has conquered death. Let the church join in the great affirmation of her faith, "I believe in . . . the resurrection of the body, and the life everlasting." —W. H. J.

Dust thou art, to dust returnest,
Was not spoken of the soul.
—Henry W. Longfellow

Flowers are the bright immortal pledge of life transcendent over death.

Immortality means living forever, with the emphasis on living.

The soul enters heaven when heaven enters the soul.

God is omnipotent, and man is immortal. Therefore be patient and work. The end shall certainly be joy, not sorrow. The stone shall roll away and the dead come forth.
—Phillips Brooks

SPECIAL DAYS AND OCCASIONS

We shall not know what life is until we die! Death is not a descent, but a never-ending ascent into the larger spaces and the fuller delights.
—J. Ossian Davies

There is only one way to get ready for immortality, and that is to love this life and live it as bravely and faithfully, and cheerfully as we can.
—Henry van Dyke

If the Father deigns to touch with divine power the cold and pulseless heart of the buried acorn and make it burst forth from its prison walls, will He leave neglected the soul of man, who was made in the image of his Creator?

No wonder that Easter is a time of joy and gladness. It celebrates the bringing of life and immortality to light; the scattering of the haze and mists of sweet fancies and beautiful guesses, and the shining forth in all its noonday brilliancy of the Sun of Righteousness; the enthronement in our hearts of a blessed certainty, which neither death, nor musty tombs, nor aught else can ever again dim.
—*The Christian World*

We must have the immortal life here and now if we would have a rational hope to have it hereafter.
—Lyman Abbott

I feel in myself the future life. I am rising, I know, toward the sky. The sunshine is over my head. Heaven lights me with the reflection of unknown worlds. . . . Winter may be on my head but eternal spring is in my heart. —Victor Hugo

He who, from zone to zone,
Guides through the boundless sky thy certain flight,
In the long way that I must tread alone,
Will lead my steps aright.
—William Cullen Bryant

Love met us and prepared the way when we came into this life; similarly love meets us when we pass into the next life and prepares the way for us there. —Borden P. Bowne

Faith in a hereafter is as necessary for the intellectual as for the moral character. —Robert Southey

The grave itself is but a covered bridge leading from light to light through a brief darkness.
—Henry W. Longfellow

God is conqueror—that is what the resurrection declares. God is conqueror—that is what life confirms. The faith by which we live is faith in a conquering God. —Albert E. Day, in
The Faith We Live

Our Lord has written the promise of the Resurrection, not in books alone, but in every leaf in springtime.
—Martin Luther

When I get to heaven, I shall see three wonders there—the first wonder will be to see many people there whom I did not expect to see; the second wonder will be to miss many people whom I did expect to see; and the third and greatest wonder of all will be to find myself there. —John Newton

The tomb is not a blind alley; it is a thoroughfare. —Victor Hugo

MOTHER'S DAY
CHRISTIAN FAMILY WEEK

A little house well filled,
A little field well tilled, and
A little wife well willed,
Are great riches.
—Grete Herbell, 1561

He is happiest, be he king or peasant, who finds his happiness at home. —Goethe

Mothers write on the hearts of their children what the world's rough hand cannot erase.

The parent problem is about to surpass the child problem.

A modern home is one where about everything is controlled by switches except the children. —Rose Green

Home is where the heart is.
—Pliny

It is a wise father who knows his own child. —Shakespeare

There are married failures, but that does not prove that marriage is a failure.

Families that pray together stay together.

The child's first school is the family.

The home worth living in is one where each lives for all, and all live for God.

Home—the place where we grumble the most and are loved the best.

Home—the place where the great are small and the small are great.

Home—a world of strife shut out, a world of love shut in.

The true home is built not by the hands but by the heart.

A small house can hold as much happiness as a big one.

All work and no play on the part of parents often leads to all play and no work on the part of the children.

The average home is just where and just what the mother makes it. The furnishings may in their texture be determined by the purse of the father, but the color scheme, the cleanliness, the sanctity—all are expressed by the maternal side. —*Christian Register*

Men are what their mothers make them. —Ralph Waldo Emerson

The only babies in a good many modern homes meow and bark.

A good example by the older generation is the best safeguard for the younger generation.

Divorce records show that many married couples spend too much time in court and not enough time in courting.

Wanted—More parents who take their children to Sunday school and church instead of sending them.

The church, more than anything else, makes and maintains the home as a place of virtue, love, righteousness, comfort, and happiness.

House rent being so high now, it is queer that people don't stay home more in order to get their money's worth.
—*Sumter Daily Item*

Every human being should have three homes: a domestic home, a church home, and an eternal home.

The big question in many American homes is, "Where are we going tonight?"

Greater love hath no parent for a child than the one who deems a good name and Christian character the finest legacy to be left behind.

> Better single still
> Than wedded ill.
> —C. H. Spurgeon

Many a fine house is something else —and less—than a home.

> I feel that, in the Heavens above,
>   The angels, whispering to one another,
> Can find, among their burning terms of love,
>   None so devotional as that of "Mother."
> —Edgar Allan Poe

Most of all the other beautiful things in life come by twos and threes, by dozens and hundreds. Plenty of roses, stars, sunsets, brothers and sisters, aunts and cousins, but only one mother in all the wide world.
—Kate Douglas Wiggin

No greater love than mother love ever existed except in the heart of God.

Mother is the name of God in the lips and hearts of little children.
—W. M. Thackeray

An ounce of mother is worth a pound of clergy. —Spanish Proverb

The trouble with home life is that so many homes have become just filling stations.

Young people, make much of it while yet you have that most precious of all good gifts, a loving mother. ... In after life you may have friends, fond, dear, kind friends; but never will you have again the inexpressible love and gentleness lavished upon you which none but a mother bestows.
—Lord Macaulay

When I was a youth I tried my best to be an infidel; but the memory of my mother's beautiful and eloquent Christianity was too much for me. I had no answer for that.
—Richard Cecil

Much of the work of mothers is done in quietness and obscurity, but it is done with patience and faithfulness. Appreciation is not always forthcoming, but the mother finds her compensation in the assurance that duty has been well done. —W. J. Hart

I owe a great deal to my mother. She was a seamstress, cook, washlady, and never until late in life had a servant in the house. And yet she was a cultivated woman. She kept up with the literature of the day. When I was a little tot she used to read good books to me. —Andrew Carnegie

No nation is better than the home life of its people.

Stay, stay at home, my heart, and rest;
Home-keeping hearts are happiest.
—Henry W. Longfellow

Home is the one place in all the world where hearts are sure of each other. It is the place of confidence. It is the spot where expressions of tenderness gush out without any sensation of awkwardness and without any dread of ridicule.—F. W. Robertson

The average family wants less outgo and more income, and the way to get it is by less go-out and more stay-in.

The hearthstone is still the cornerstone of the nation.

The world needs brother love as well as mother love.

Family scraps may be the result of scrapping the family altar.

No matter how palatial the home in which we live, we still dwell in tents —content or discontent.
—*Pittsburgh Christian Advocate*

Money can build a house, but it takes love to make it a home.

The right temperature at home is more surely maintained by the warm hearts and cool heads of those who live there than by electric thermostats.

Is your home a place of rest and refreshment where God Himself becomes more real to those who enter it?
—*Friends Book of Discipline*

The path of a good woman is indeed strewn with flowers; but they rise behind her steps, not before them.
—John Ruskin

PENTECOST

The serene, silent beauty of a holy life is the most powerful influence in the world, next to the might of the Spirit of God. —C. H. Spurgeon

Modern Christians too often want their religion thinned down, sweetened up and sprayed upon. ... But vital Christianity is radical and revolutionary. It is dynamite.
—O. Walter Wagner

The Spirit bears fruit only if rooted in a pious life.

Enough spiritual power is going to waste to put a thousand Niagaras to shame.

Pentecost was preceded by penitence, piety, prayer, and power.

Quick Quotes for Church Bulletins

Pentecost was preceded by prayer, precipitated by prayer, and can only be perpetuated by prayer.

Pentecost is great enough, important enough, and inspiring enough to be commemorated with all earnestness and devotion throughout all Christendom.

Prayerless pews make powerless pulpits.

Christ lived in the flesh so that He might show us how to live in the Spirit.

Easter is perfected in Pentecost.

If we take God's program we can have God's power—not otherwise.
—E. Stanley Jones

We have been too dull to see and too unchristian to follow out the implications of Pentecost.
—E. Stanley Jones

At Pentecost all life, language, culture, national genius, art, science, philosophy—all life is gathered into a common center, Christ, and then it goes out from that common center to tell, each in its own language, the wonderful works of God.
—E. Stanley Jones

The miracle of transformed lives is the best evidence of the gospel's power.

Nothing lies beyond the power of man if it lies within the will of God.

The real function of the religion of Jesus is not merely to show men how they ought to live, but to supply the power necessary for one to live that way.

The Church fulfills its holy purpose only as it is filled with the Holy Ghost.

The Holy Spirit came on the Day of Pentecost:
In a sound, to awaken them;
In a wind, to move them;
In fire, to enlighten and warm them;
In tongues, to make them speak.

Two men were gazing at Niagara Falls. One remarked: "The greatest unused power in the world."
The other replied: "Not so, the greatest unused power in the world is the Holy Spirit of the living God."
—W. H. Stewart

"With one accord in one place." This unity had much to do with the gift of the Holy Spirit. "To separate ourselves from our brethren is to lose power. Half-dead brands heaped close will kindle one another. Fling them apart and they go out. Pull them together and they glow." —A. Maclaren

On the Day of Pentecost the coming of the Spirit upon a company of waiting disciples changed them from an aggregation of units into one corporate whole, the Church of the living God. —G. Campbell Morgan

One of the outcomes of a Spirit-filled life is a new illumination to understand God's Word. —F. E. Marsh

The fires of the Holy Spirit consume "the rags of self-righteousness, the leaves of an empty profession, the stubble of questioning doubt, the thorns of prickly temper, the filth of unholy desire, the chaff of useless endeavor, the roots of black bitterness, the straw of pretentious unreality, and the refuse of unprofitable talk."
—F. E. Marsh

He who speaks of heavenly things speaks with new tongues.—Gregory

If any man have not the Spirit of Christ, he is none of his.
—Romans 8:9

A form of godliness, without the power thereof, is the chief blemish on Christ's Church.

I sought Thee at a distance, and did not know that Thou wast near. I sought Thee abroad in Thy works, and behold, Thou wast in me.
—Augustine

VACATION TIME

Character is what a man is while on his vacation.

The devil usually eases up his work when the church takes a vacation. He can afford to.

Spiritual food is needed in hot weather as well as in cool.

"Remember the Sabbath Day to keep it holy" applies to vacation Sundays as well as the rest of the year.

You expect God's grace in summer as well as in winter. Has He not a right to your all-year-round devotion?

What if God were to take a vacation in His care of you?

A vacation is a short duration of recreation, preceded by a period of anticipation and followed by a period of recuperation.

It might be easier to mobilize the church if it were not already automobilized.

One of the most enjoyable features of a summer vacation is the thrill of getting back home after it is over.

When one goes on a vacation, there are two things that ought not to be left behind—common sense and religion. You will have need of both.

Granting that it is possible to worship God in the woods and the fields, it is well to bear in mind that there is a difference between true worship and just enjoying the landscape.

Never take a vacation from God.

Satan finds some mischief still for idle hands to do.—Isaac Watts.

The devil always shows up at vacation resorts, but that does not mean he is on vacation.

It's pretty hard to take a vacation from doing nothing.

When the church takes a vacation, the devil may safely take his.

Temptation rarely comes in working hours. It is in their leisure time that men are made or marred.
—W. M. Taylor

An idler is a watch that wants both hands,
As useless if it goes as if it stands.
—William Cowper

LABOR DAY

What is morally wrong cannot be economically right.

All work and no play makes Jack a dull boy—and his dad a dull man.

President Lincoln once was asked by an aristocratic lady if the Lincoln family had a coat of arms.
"Yes, indeed," replied the ex-rail-splitter. "It's a pair of shirt sleeves. Would you like to see them?"

Part of religion's business is to make business more religious.

To succeed is easier than to make alibis for failure.

The best way to be done with duty is to discharge it.

Many a man has to keep his nose to the grindstone so his wife can keep hers turned up at the neighbors.

That which is everybody's business is nobody's business.—Isaac Watts

Whatever is worth doing at all is worth doing well.
—The Earl of Chesterfield

What this country needs is more tractors and fewer detractors.

The best preparation for tomorrow is to make good use of today.

In labors of love every day is pay day.

The use one makes of his leisure hours often determines the value of his working hours.

The person who is content to be a leaner will likely become leaner and leaner.

One cannot waste time. He simply wastes his life.

Man's chief business in the world, whether he be a day laborer or a captain of industry, is to build a life and through it have a definite part in building the Kingdom of God.

Those who try to float to success will end up at sea.

Don't be discouraged by failure or satisfied with success.

One day Fortune actually knocked on a fellow's door. But the fellow didn't hear it; he was at a neighbor's telling a hard-luck story.

The ambition to do well is far better than the ambition to be well-to-do.

It may be true the willing horse gets the heaviest load, but he also develops the strongest muscles and generally gets the most oats.

The elevator to success is not running; you must climb the stairs.

Everything that is worth while is up grade.

The sort of ships that come in while we sit and wait usually are hardships.

God must like common people or He would not have made so many of them.
—Abraham Lincoln

The sweetest lives are those to duty wed.—Elizabeth Barrett Browning

Get thy tools ready; God will find thee work.   —Robert Browning

The best angle with which to approach any problem is the try-angle.

When we become partners with God in His work, He becomes a partner with us in our work.

More than any other institution, the church sympathizes with the weak, the wronged and oppressed, and pleads for social justice.

We are labourers together with God.
—I Corinthians 3:9

The more you wait for something to turn up, the more liable you are to get turned down.

About the best method of climbing higher is to remain on the level.
—*North Adams Herald*

"I believe I could make a better world than this myself," growled a dissatisfied man.
To which his friend answered cheerfully: "Sure, that's what you're here for. Get to work!"   —*Forward*

Moses was a labor leader, but he collected no dues.

One of these days men will not only be ordained to the ministry, but ordained to whatever job they decide to take up, for all service to the community is service to God.
—Leslie D. Weatherhead

A cobbler, a smith, a peasant, every man, has the office and function of his calling, and yet all alike are consecrated priests and bishops and every man in his office may be useful and beneficial to the rest, that so many kinds of work may be united in one community, just as the members of a body all serve one another.
—Martin Luther

A young man once wrote to Henry Ward Beecher, asking him to find an "easy place" for him. Beecher replied: "You cannot be an editor; do not try the law; do not think of the ministry; let alone all ships, shops, and merchandise; be not a farmer nor a mechanic; neither be a soldier nor a sailor; don't work, don't study, don't think. Oh, my son, you have come into a hard world!

I know of only one easy place in it, and that is the grave."

The Sunday-school teacher asked: "Are there any idols in America?"
A small boy replied: "Yes, my father and my uncle are idle."

Easy Street has a dead end.

It is unlikely there will be a reduction in the wages of sin.

He who does what he should will not have time to do what he should not.

Success is 2 per cent genius and 98 per cent honest effort.
—Thomas A. Edison

If there be lying before you any bit of work from which you shrink, go straight up to it! The best way to get rid of it is to do it. In every piece of honest work, however irksome, laborious or commonplace, we are fellow-laborers with God.
—F. B. Meyer

Give us the man who sings at his work, be his occupation what it may—he is equal to any of those who follow the same pursuit in silence and sullenness. He will do more in the same time and will do it better. He will preserve longer.
—Thomas Carlyle

There is no sweeter repose than that which is brought with labor.

If you are so busy you cannot stop and think, you had better stop and think.

Motion is two thirds of promotion.

Between the great things we can't do and the little things we won't do, the danger is we shall do nothing.

The danger in this modern age is that many are "better off" without being better.

God provides food for every bird, but he does not throw it into the nest.

The person who is idle simply because he does not have to work is merely a respectable hobo.

The most unprofitable item ever manufactured is an excuse.

Yes, a lot of fellows never had a chance—and the Wright brothers never had an airplane until they made one. Get the idea?

Thank God every morning when you get up that you have something to do that day which must be done whether you like it or not. Being forced to work, and forced to do your best, will breed in you a hundred virtues which the idle never know.
—Charles Kingsley

Horse sense means knowing how to pull, when to pull back, and how to work with a teammate.

Get the pattern of your life from God, and then go about your work and be yourself.—Phillips Brooks

A nation that makes things, and cannot make men to match those things, is a failure.
—Margaret Slattery

All things will come to the other fellow if you sit down and wait.

Let not him who is houseless pull down the house of another, but let him work diligently and build one for himself, thus by example assuring that his own shall be safe from violence when built.   —Abraham Lincoln

In America the dignity of labor is recognized, and it is idleness rather than toil that is felt to be a disgrace. This is a direct fruit of the religion that presents the Son of God and the Saviour of men as working at the carpenter's bench, and His leading followers as men that earned their bread by working with their hands.

The trouble with most of the people who sit and wait for their ships to come in is they have never launched

any ships to begin with. We must build and launch, before sitting down to expect return cargoes.
—*The Christian Age*

A Labor Day Prayer. Dignify our common toil, O Carpenter of Nazareth, with ideals of service, insight of real values, inhibitions of self-belittlement, impulses of affection, inspiring songs of hope and industrious patience. Amen. —Christian F. Reisner

Pegging away
Will win the day.
—C. H. Spurgeon

You don't get much done by starting tomorrow.

The darkest hour in any man's life is when he sits down to plan how to get money without earning it.
—Horace Greeley

Success is sweet, but its secret is sweat.

Opportunity seldom knocks at the door of a knocker.—*Cleveland Press*

What this country needs is not so much a job for every man, but a real man for every job.

Diamonds are chunks of coal that stuck to their jobs.

Nothing is worth the making if it does not make the man.
—Edwin Markham

The secret of life is not so much to do what one likes, but to like what one does. —John Ruskin

Too many people itch for what they want but are unwilling to get out and scratch for it.

Too much time is wasted by some people in telling how busy they are.

The highest reward that God gives us for good work is the ability to do better. —Elbert Hubbard

Every blade of grass is a study; and to produce two where there was but one is both a profit and a pleasure.
—Abraham Lincoln

No men living are more worthy to be trusted than those who toil up from poverty. —Abraham Lincoln

Start where you are with what you have; make something of it; never be satisfied.
—George Washington Carver

God helps those who help themselves.
—Algernon Sidney

The father of success is Work.

It would be better for some self-made men if the job had been done by someone else.

Even the woodpecker owes his success to the fact that he uses his head and keeps pecking away until he finishes the job he starts.
—Coleman Cox

If you are made wretched by another person's prosperity, you need something besides money.

That man stated a bigger truth than he knew when he said about his home town: "This is the starting point for any place in the world. You can start here and go anywhere you want to."

The aristocracy of race and birth must give way to the aristocracy of worth.

The weekly rest day for the toiler is a gift from Christianity, and the maintenance of the Sabbath depends on the strength of Christian influence. For the workingman himself to misuse it or allow it to be attacked in his name would be like a man's sawing off the branch on which he is sitting.

When Jesus chose His disciples, He selected busy men, but not too busy to put first things first.

Don't put things off—put them over.

The door of opportunity is marked, *"push."*

Even the woodpecker has discovered the only way to succeed is to use one's head.

Genius is one per cent inspiration and ninety-nine per cent perspiration.
—Thomas A. Edison

Even if you are on the right track, you will get run over if you just sit there.

If you want something done, ask a busy man to do it.—Elbert Hubbard

Two elements of success: aspire, then perspire.

Many of us could have the things we wish we had, if we didn't spend half of our time wishing for them.
—Alexander Woollcott

The devil has no unemployment problem.

Drudgery is as necessary to call out the treasures of the mind as harrowing and planting those of the earth.
—Margaret Fuller

When love and skill work together, expect a masterpiece.—John Ruskin

Let the farmer be forevermore honored in his calling; for they who labor in the earth are the chosen people of God. —Thomas Jefferson

If you write a better book, or preach a better sermon, or build a better mousetrap than your neighbor, the world will make a beaten path to your door. —Ralph Waldo Emerson

Contentment lies not in the enjoyment of ease—a life of luxury—but comes only to him that labors and overcomes—to him that performs the task in hand and reaps the satisfaction of work well done.
—Oscar Wilde

I once had a wise old commander who used to say: "Always take your job seriously—never yourself."
—Dwight D. Eisenhower

The way a man handles other men is not half so important as the way a man handles himself.

Nothing is more dangerous than idleness. He who has nothing to do will soon be doing something wrong. Our idle days are Satan's busy days.

Jesus taught by action. . . . He did not discourse on the dignity of labor—He worked at a carpenter's bench and His hands were hard with the toil of making yokes and plows, and this forever makes the toil of the hands honorable. —E. Stanley Jones

REFORMATION

It has been said that the Reformation was born in Luther's prayer closet. All reformation, individual and collective, begins in someone's prayer closet. —E. Stanley Jones

Prayer changes things.

More things are wrought by prayer Than this world dreams of.
—Alfred, Lord Tennyson

Faith is not belief without proof but trust without reservations.
—Elton Trueblood

The truth shall make you free.
—Jesus

It is better to light a candle than to curse the darkness.

Life is surely given us for higher purposes than to gather what our ancestors wisely have thrown away.
—Samuel Johnson

The day Martin Luther threw the ink pot at the devil he missed him, but he was a better marksman with the pen.

As a shoemaker makes a shoe, and a tailor a coat, so must the Christian

pray. A Christian's work is prayer.
—Martin Luther

We no more earn heaven by good works than babies earn their food and drink by crying and howling.
—Martin Luther

Christ's Word will I defend with happy heart and fresh courage, afraid of no one; thereto has God given me a happy and intrepid spirit.
—Martin Luther

Paul never said, "I know *what* I believe," but, "I know *whom* I believe." —C. R. Scoville

"Here I stand," said Martin Luther. But he didn't just stand; he went places and did things.

If I rest, I rust.
—Martin Luther, *Maxims*

We must discriminate between innovation and renovation. Reformations are simply revivals of truth lost sight of, or buried under the rubbish of error. —A. J. Gordon

Protestants believe:
Our spiritual authority is in the Bible.
All believers have direct access to God.
We are justified by faith.
Every Christian should read the Holy Scriptures, try to understand them, and live up to the dictates of an enlightened conscience.
There are two vital and necessary sacraments—Baptism and the Lord's Supper.
Church and state should be separate, but not exclusive of each other.
As Christians believing in the freedom of conscience, and as Americans believing in our national traditions, we are deeply and resolutely committed to the separation of church and state as a sound principle verified by our own experience.
—Bulletin, National Council of Churches

F-A-I-T-H means, *F*orsaking *A*ll *I* *T*ake *H*im. —Phillips Brooks

In realm after realm, experience teaches us that life, to be safe and good, must have the support of sound convictions. And surely the realm of religion is no exception.

Let us as Protestants take pride in our great traditions and cling to them. Since our souls have direct access to God, let us freely practice His presence at all times. Let us read the Book which is the authority for life; and let us stand fast in the freedom wherewith Christ has set us free.
—Albea Godbold

The Protestant is just as much the heir of all the Christian centuries as is the Catholic. Protestantism, in its essential nature, began with Jesus, not with the Reformers. St. Paul set forth in the first century what Luther and Calvin reaffirmed in the sixteenth. . . . Protestant and Catholic have a common substructure under their feet.—Samuel McCrea Cavert

I cannot and I will not recant anything. . . . Here I stand, I cannot do otherwise. God help me. Amen.
—Martin Luther

I am in earnest! I will not equivocate! I will not excuse: I will not retreat a single inch! And I will be heard! —William Lloyd Garrison

One, on God's side, is a majority.
—Wendell Phillips

The best reformers the world has ever known are those who began with themselves. —George Bernard Shaw

THANKSGIVING

Giving thanks means little unless you are living thanks.

When you think, you will thank.

It is better to speak of benefits received rather than of those you bestow.

No one really gives thanks unless he is willing to give more than thanks.

How sharper than a serpent's tooth it is.
To have a thankless child.
—or father, or mother, or brother, or sister, or. . . .

Great as were the preparations for the dinner, everything was so contrived that not a soul in the house should be kept from the morning service of Thanksgiving in the church.
—Harriet Beecher Stowe, in *Old Town Folks*

Let us be ever thankful for the church of our forebears, remembering those who founded it. Let us remember also those who during the succeeding decades maintained it, enlarged it, beautified it, and enriched it with their labors. Let us dedicate ourselves to follow in their way.

Learn to appreciate the good things that you have and you will not miss the good things you haven't.
—*Religious Telescope*

If Christians praised God more the world would doubt Him less.
—Charles E. Jefferson

A thankful heart doubles our blessings, causing us to enjoy them twice —when we receive them, and when we remember them.

Thanksgiving is the vibration of the soul's heartstrings under the soft touch of God's benevolence.

God's greatness hath been great to thee.
Let never day nor night unhallowed pass,
But still remember what the Lord hath done.
—Shakespeare

Ingratitude curdles the milk of human kindness.

Do you not teach your children to say "Thank you" for what they receive? Well, we are the children of God, and He demands of us that we shall not take anything He gives as a matter of course, but in a spirit of thankfulness. —Baring-Gould

If the Pilgrim Fathers, with so few temporal blessings to brighten their privations, could be so thankful, shall we not by prayer and supplication make known to God, and the world, our gratitude for our numberless blessings?

Some people grumble because God placed thorns among roses, yet never thank Him for the roses among the thorns.

We can be thankful in a topsy-turvy world if our own lives are right side up.

Let us be thankful on Thanksgiving Day! Nature is beautiful; fellowmen are dear; duty is close beside us; and God is over all. —Phillips Brooks

When our little personal world or the world about us seems to be breaking up, we should remember what we once had; think more deeply of what we still have; and the flow of thanksgiving will grow into a stream.
—Vincent L. Bennett

The greatest possession for which to be thankful is a thankful heart.

True thanksgiving is a cultivated habit rather than an occasional emphasis.

If you can think of nothing for which to give thanks, you have a poor memory.

One cannot pay God in money for His goodness. The coin of grateful praise is what reaches the heart of God.

O, for a thousand tongues to sing
  My great Redeemer's praise,
begins a Wesleyan hymn. Many yearn for a thousand tongues with which to praise God yet poorly use the one tongue they have.

Many of us grumble because we are temporarily deprived of blessings our forefathers never even heard of.

Once more the liberal year laughs out
　O'er richer stores than gems of gold;
Once more with harvest-song and shout
　Is Nature's bloodless triumph told.
　　　—Whittier, "Harvest Hymn"

There is danger of leaving God out of our Thanksgiving Day. We are making it a holiday rather than a holy day. It is a day for the public recognition of God as the giver of all good. To leave God out of Thanksgiving Day is as absurd as leaving Christ out of Christmas.

Ingratitude is not only the basest and meanest of sins, but it is the most frequent.
　　　—Wilton Merle Smith

When troubles come, go at them with songs. When griefs arise, sing them down. Lift the voice of praise against cares.
　　　—Henry Ward Beecher

A thankful spirit is like sunshine upon the fields.

ADVENT AND CHRISTMAS

A Christless Christmas is something else—and less—than Christmas.

Christmas began in the heart of God. It is complete only when it reaches the heart of man.
　　　—*Religious Telescope*

Christmas services must not take the place of Christmas service.

God's love gave Christmas to the world, and only that love in human hearts can keep Christmas in the world.

Christmas at its best means the enthronement of Jesus Christ in the human heart.

God so loved the world that He gave His only begotten Son as a Christmas gift, that whosoever believes in him, and accepts Him as Saviour, should not perish, but have everlasting life.

Because Jesus was born in a manger is no reason we should make the church look like a barn.

The angels broke into song when Jesus came. So to every life, song comes with the coming of Jesus into it.

Don't be too harsh with the Bethlehem innkeeper, especially if Christ is not given a central place in your heart and home.

It is the glory of Christianity that it not only reveals God *for* us, and God *with* us, but God *in* us.

The richest and sweetest joys human hearts can experience were born into the world when Christ was born.

The Incarnation is simply a great object-lesson of God's love. He loved before, but the Incarnation taught men that He loved and how much He loved.

It is Christmas in the heart that puts Christmas in the air.
　　　—W. T. Ellis

The Wise Men sought Christ, which proves they were wise men.

Where there is heart-room there also is house-room.—Celtic Proverb

Always, "There's a song in the air:" when Christmas comes.

When the Babe of Bethlehem is born in your heart, you will not ask how to sing—you'll just sing, whether on the key or off it.

Christmas creates "one great fellowship of love throughout the whole wide earth."

Don't become so busy celebrating Christmas that you have no time for Christ.

That the Wise Men were wise men is shown by their willingness to suffer hardship and inconvenience in order to worship Christ.

> O Rest beside the weary road,
> And hear the angels sing!

The Christmas bells some like best are on cash registers.

It was said that the Wise Men after visiting the Babe in the manger "went back another way." No one can really see Christ and go back the same way. Life becomes different from that hour.
—E. Stanley Jones

It is not enough to prepare your home and your pantry for Christmas. "Let every heart prepare Him room."

Christ says: "Behold, I stand at the door, and knock." Will you open the door of your heart and your home to Him, or will you, like the Bethlehem innkeeper, hang out the "No Vacancy" sign?

God in Christ became the Son of man that we might become the sons of God.

If Christ had not come, there would not be a Christian in the whole world. Imagine that!

Christ is the fulfillment of all hopes, the perfection of all philosophy, the interpretation of all revelation, the key to all the seeming contradictions of the physical and moral world.

Christmas is the season for kindling the fire of hospitality in the hall, the genial flame of charity in the heart.
—Washington Irving

I will honor Christmas in my heart, and try to keep it all the year.
—Charles Dickens

Put Christ back into Christmas.

Your greatest Christmas cheer comes when you dispense cheer.

> God is not dead, nor doth he sleep!
> The wrong shall fail,
> The right prevail,
> With peace on earth, good will to men!
> —Henry W. Longfellow

Since God has appeared in a manger, should we be surprised to find him anywhere?

If Christ has really taken up his abode in a human heart, often he will be seen looking out of the windows.
—*China's Millions*

Special Christmas Menu: Grace—Kindness—Bread of Life—Living Water—Sweet Thoughts—Tender Memories — Heart (Whole) — Happiness (Unmeasured)—Cup of Joy (Running Over)—Charity (Served with Discretion)—Fruits of the Spirit.

"Thanks be unto God for his unspeakable gift!"—II Corinthians 9:15

Warm your Christmas heart at the altar of your church.

The earth has grown old with its burden of care, but at Christmas it always is young.

The manger at Bethlehem and the carpenter's shop at Nazareth cast a glow of celestial glory over the humble and the commonplace.

When Christ was born, the angel choir hovering over the fields of Bethlehem opened the doors of heaven and let the sweetest and richest music out to flood the earth through all time.

Many observe Christmas but do not keep it. Observance lasts for a day, but keeping it in our hearts lasts through the year.

Christ's estimate of the value of little children is in His own words, "Of such is the kingdom of heaven." Someone has queried, "Who could have foretold, when Jesus was born, what He would become?"

Look over your Christmas giving list. Be honest now, will the best gift you give be to Him whose birthday it is?

Go slow thinking harsh thoughts of the Bethlehem innkeeper, if you have no place in your heart and home for Christ today.

Jesus came, not to hush the natural music of men's lives, nor to fill it with storm and agitation, but to retune every silver chord in that "harp of a thousand strings" and to make it echo with the harmonies of heaven.
—Frederic W. Farrar

Earth grows into heaven, as we come to live and breathe in the atmosphere of the incarnation. Jesus makes heaven wherever He is.
—F. W. Faber

Chapter II

Church Attendance—The Sabbath—Christian Worship and Work

The height of the church spire is not as important as how high the church members aspire.

You are not related to Christ by being a brother-in-law to the church.

One doesn't have to go to church in order to be good, but good people want to go to church.

This church does not seek to impose a creed, but to share a life.

Sunday is Christ's election day. If His purposes are defeated, it will be because of the stay-at-homes who failed to vote.

Prayer is fundamental, not supplemental.

Cultivation of the soil is not as important as the cultivation of the soul.

Prayer is the connecting link between this life and that which is soon to be.

Religion is not a fur coat to be put away in moth balls during the summer months.—*Baptist Reminder*, Dallas, Texas.

Nothing is discussed more and practiced less than prayer.

The right way to begin traveling the right way is to begin right away.

People seldom lose their religion by a "blow-out." Usually it is just a "slow leak." —Otis Moore

One man says: "I do not go to church on Sunday because I was never taught to go when I was young, so I did not form the habit." Another man says: "I do not go to church on Sunday because I was forced to go when I was young and it grew distasteful to me." One excuse is as good as another when you do not want to do a thing. —*The Watchman Examiner*

God calls. No answer is a "No" answer.

The feeblest knock will open heaven's door.

Religion is neither a winter resort nor a last resort.

Where do we go from here? Let's go to church!

God wants a whole heart, but will accept a broken one.

A prayer is merely a wish turned heavenward.

Prayer is not conquering God's reluctance, but taking hold of God's willingness.

The man who is too busy to pray is too busy.

Each person needs something to live for apart from himself and his own work. Nothing short of participation in the sublime undertaking of the evangelization of the world is adequate to emancipate us from selfishness, and to call out the best energies of mind and heart. —John R. Mott

To "sing with the spirit and with the understanding also" requires more than a trained voice.

A revival of the Christian spirit among church members would solve many church problems.

If one expects to answer "when the roll is called up yonder," he had better be present when the roll is called down here.

Churchgoing may not be the essence of religion, but it is an evidence of religion.

Prayer is something more than asking God to run errands for us.

The devil enjoys hearing a prayer that is addressed to an audience.

Time spent in prayer is not time lost, but time gained.

Say this for the automobile—it never takes people away from church against their will.

The sermon you enjoy most is not likely to be the one that will do you the most good.

The minister's success lies not in what the people think of him, but in what he can lead them to think of Christ.

A church advertised for "used" pews. We wish ours were used more.

Your religion will do more for you if you do more for it.

No one becomes a Christian on his own terms.

There's no use going to the altar to tell God how good you are.

Formal worship does not correct a faulty life.

Our Lord is not seeking compliments, but commitments.

God will forgive those who start late in life to serve Him, but He will not forgive those who quit early. "Be thou faithful unto death."

The one guarantee of success in church work—"the people *have* a mind to work."

I have never heard anything about the "resolutions" of the Apostles, but I have heard a great deal about the Acts of the Apostles.
—Horace Mann

If you know God, you will trust Him.

Many who want God to be near when they need Him, are not close by when God needs them.

You should not pronounce it a poor sermon until you have tested it in practice.

Perhaps you can help improve your preacher's preaching by being a better listener.

Remember, your empty pew always places a question mark after your profession of faith.

The man behind the man behind the pulpit is a bigger factor in the church than he will ever know.

The great need of the church is not so much a pulpit that will draw as a pew that will radiate.

The church is not supposed to be a reservoir, but a channel of blessing.

"Not good if detached," so reads your railroad ticket. Something like that can be said of those who detach themselves from the church.

When I neglect the services of my church, I injure its good name, I lessen its power, I discourage its members, and I chill my own soul.

Christianity is not a puzzle to be solved, but a way of life to be adopted. It is not a creed to be memorized, but a Person to follow.

A cold church, like cold butter, never spreads well.

Church Attendance—The Sabbath—Christian Worship and Work

The churches of this country are its greatest bulwark against the forces that are constantly battering at the base of civilization. As a patriot and good citizen, it is your duty to support the church.

Why go to church? Because the church is God's way of saving, conserving, and keeping humanity from moral degeneration.

Take it from me: the church offers you something you just cannot get elsewhere.

A full pew is the church's best advertisement.

Let us go to church so that we will feel at home when we get to heaven.

Genuine Christians do not want to go to heaven alone.

Spirit of God, descend upon my heart;
  Wean it from earth; through all its pulses move;
Stoop to my weakness, mighty as Thou art,
  And make me love Thee as I ought to love.
—George Croly

To hear the call of God, one must be within hearing distance.

"Remember the Sabbath day to keep it holy." Otherwise we may forget we are Christians.

You will enjoy the service more if you do not sit in the seat of the scornful.

Some say, "the Church." Some say, "my church." What do you say?

The purpose of prayer is not to change the Divine will, but to adjust oneself to it. —Frank Crane

Go to church to get away from yourself.

Don't stay away from church because it is not perfect. How lonely you would feel in a perfect church!

Daily prayers lessen daily cares.

A committee of five usually consists of the man who does the work, two to pat him on the back, and two to bring in a minority report.
—Rialb Leumas

Prayer lubricates the machinery of life.

True religion is never solitary.

The Church is not an art gallery for exhibition of eminent Christians, but a school for the education of imperfect ones. —H. W. Beecher

Friends are life's priceless treasure; he who has none is a social pauper.

The best way to get rid of an enemy is to make a friend of him.

This church flings wide its doors like welcoming arms and invites you to come in. This is your Father's house. Why should not one feel at home and welcome in the house of his Father?

Let us not come into this auditorium for the purpose of enjoying ourselves, or for listening to good music, or for hearing sermons. Let us come to worship Almighty God, our great Father; to exalt the name of Jesus Christ, our great Saviour; and to listen to the silent voice of the Holy Spirit, our great Guide.

Someone rises to remark that the attendance at the morning service tests the popularity of the church; the attendance at the evening service tests the popularity of the minister; and the attendance at prayer meeting tests the popularity of the Lord.

Now is the time for all good men, women, boys, and girls to come to the aid of their church.

There are some in every congregation who merely receive the sermon and place it on file.
—Oliver Wendell Holmes

The word "revival" comes from the Latin *revivere*, to live again. Well, that is just what some individuals and churches need.

He who doesn't believe anything is not likely to do anything—that is, anything worth doing.

Some church members are standbyers and some are by-standers.

We are happiest in the Lord's work when we are so busy that we don't even think of happiness.

Someone suggests that when you've tried everything else, try religion. Why not try religion first? It would save the trouble of trying everything else.

Some strain at a drizzle at the hour for a church service, and swallow a shower at theater time.

The man who wants to get rid of the Sabbath because it is ancient, to be consistent ought to reject the sunshine.

God works through people who work.

The empty-pew problem is not solved when the pew is occupied by a person with a wandering mind.

We can endure the long and rugged road if it leads to the place of blessing.

A poor listener seldom hears a good sermon.

Dry hearing is responsible for much dry preaching.

Christian talk is no substitute for the Christian walk.

If you want to get away from hypocrites, better seek the Kingdom of God and His righteousness. There'll be no hypocrites in heaven.

What are we called upon to leave when we follow Christ? Only those things which work against our own soul's welfare—the sins of the world, the selfishness of our lower nature, our fears, our sloth.
—Frederick L. Fagley

When one becomes a Christian, he takes up infinitely more than he gives up.

Church members often are weakened by too much week end.

When your religion gets into the past tense, it becomes pretense.

One way to defend your church is to attend its services.

Some would find it easier to keep faith sweet and strong if they used it more.

Blessed is the man who loves his church enough to let others know it.

Breathe on me, breath of God,
  Till I am wholly Thine,
Till all this earthly part of me
  Glows with Thy fire divine.
—Edwin Hatch

Conversion is that change, sudden or gradual, by which we pass from the kingdom of self to the Kingdom of God, through the grace and power of Jesus Christ. —E. Stanley Jones

Many church members are like the farmer's well. It had only two faults: it froze up in winter-time and dried up in the summer-time.
—*The Watchman-Examiner*

If our church is to be a going concern, we must have churchgoing members.

The frost of sin often nips spiritual greatness in the bud.

We should not bring a Saturday mind to a Sunday service.

Of course you respect the church, but do you prove it to your children by attending? Actions speak louder than words.

The organ prelude is a veil dropped between every-day life and the sanctuary; in crossing the threshold, the music should separate the world without from the world within. Let us cease our conversation with each other and use the organ period for quiet meditation and communion with God.
—Bulletin, St. Mark's Methodist Church, Baltimore

Some people think they are keeping the Sabbath by merely putting on their best clothes.

A church spire is symbolic. It is a finger pointing upward to the Power above us, from which we derive our spiritual strength. It marks a building as a place where we gather for a communion that renews our faith.

Instead of waiting on the Lord, some expect the Lord to wait on them.

The man who uses Sunday only to sleep, to loaf around the house, to read secular papers, to do a few odd jobs needing attention, and to take a joy-ride places a mighty small valuation upon, not the church, but his own soul.

"Now I lay me down to sleep" seems to be the prayer some pray just as the service is about to begin.

To really enjoy religion, one must first have it, then use it.

Call the police! The choir murdered the anthem, the organist drowned the choir, the preacher butchered his English, and the janitor smothered the congregation.

Do your bit where you are. If the world doesn't see you, it makes no difference; God does.

One time when we ought to make a special effort to pray is when we don't feel like it.

The church has suffered from putting too high a premium on orthodoxy in words and too little emphasis upon superiority in deeds and character.
—*Advance*

Keep your Sundays for the great things of the soul.

After the service some get out of the church as though the benediction were a fire alarm and they were firemen on duty.

The church should be the Society of the Forgiven and Forgiving.
—W. G. Spencer

The very worst calamity which could befall any human being would be this—to have his own way from the cradle to the grave; to have everything he liked for the asking, or even for the buying. Never to deny himself, never to work, never to exert himself, never to want. That man's soul would be in as great danger as if he were committing great crimes.
—Charles Kingsley

C-H-U-R-C-H spells Church. But it doesn't mean anything unless UR in it.

If we claim God as our Father, we should be willing to act like His children.

What is Christianity? In the home, it is kindness; in business, it is honesty; in society, it is courtesy; in work, it is thoroughness; in play, it is fairness; toward the fortunate, it is congratulation; toward the unfortunate, it is pity; toward the weak, it is help; toward the wicked, it is resistance; toward the strong, it is trust; toward the penitent, it is forgiveness; and toward God, it is reverence and love. —Douglas Hyde

Not what you think of the preacher, but what you think of Christ, is the measure of your strength in the church.

Communion Meditation. It is the duty of the Lord's people on the Lord's Day to gather around the Lord's Table.

I think it is the duty of every man to go to church. Frequently I have to listen to sermons that bore me.

But the church has contributed so enormously to civilization, its service to society is so great, that irrespective of other considerations I feel I ought to support it and to attend whenever I can. —Theodore Roosevelt

You are invited to unite with this church in the promotion of a deeper spirituality, better social conditions, and the spread of the gospel at home and abroad.

If statistics have taught me anything, it is that the biggest thing in man is not body, mind, or muscle; but soul. Wages, prices, and conditions can be adjusted; but attitudes, motives, and relationships can only be converted. —Roger Babson

Don't go home as soon as Sunday School is dismissed. Somebody might follow your example and never come back. Example is the world's best or worst teacher. Stay for the sermon. It might be the last one you will ever hear.—*Youngstown Christian News*

In the love of truth and in the spirit of Christ we are united for the worship of God and the service of man.

Sunday is the only day some people have in which there is any chance to think high and holy thoughts. What a tragedy, then, to spend it in the fruitless pastime of watching the trunk of the car ahead.
—*The Christian Advocate*

We offer a warm welcome for every worshiper, and work for all who are willing.

Don't mind if the preacher in your parish is not gifted; you can bring a large torch to a very small flame and carry away a great blaze.

The pastor has to deal with more cases of sleeping sickness than does the physician.

If the church does not miss you when you remain away from the service, it is probably a worse commentary upon you than upon the church.

You need not scoff at the church because it contains so many sinners. If it contained nothing but saints there might be no room for you. The Christian church was founded for sinners in the first place, and unless you are a saint, you need it.—H. N. Nimmo

In the name of our Lord Jesus Christ we welcome you to a place in this sanctuary. Blessed be your coming in, and blessed be your going out.

Why allow Sunday visitors to keep you at home for friendly gossip and meaningless chatter? Bring them to church on Sunday and let us do the talking.

Where there is no Christian Sabbath, there is no Christian morality; and without this, free institutions cannot long be sustained.
—Justice McLean, U. S. Supreme Court

Empty pews have a voice of their own. They cry out in solemn testimony against the people of God who are not in them.

The Sabbath is the shadow of Christ on the hot highway of time. We pause in it as in a shelter from the heat, and are refreshed.—Robert E. Speer

As a businessman I urge my associates to get behind the churches. They alone provide a solution to the great problems facing us. . . . The need of the hour is not more houses, or freight cars, not more factories or ships, not more legislation, education or banking facilities, but more religion. The need of the hour is religion.
—Roger W. Babson

If a man really gets a good case of religion, he will find that it is contagious.

To keep in good *standing* with God we must *kneel*.

The world has an overplus of men who could if they would, but won't.

Some people know Christ; some just know about Him.

The rule in the army is, "All present or accounted for." Should not the same rule be effective in the army of the Lord?

The church is the avenue through which we walk to the heights of God.

If you don't believe in co-operation, just observe what happens when one wheel of a wagon comes off.

Religion is the response of the soul to the call of God.

It feels good to be good.

The Creator did not set apart the Sabbath for the purpose of digging dandelions or greasing the car.

One cannot be loyal to Christ without being loyal to His Church.

Take one day a week to look up and away from the world, and get your bearings.

Stand with the best people for the best things. Stand with the church.

Go to church, to quiet the voice within you which says, "You ought."

Go to church, to give your soul, smothered by many worldly interests, a chance to breathe.

Be as faithful in keeping your appointments in religion as in business.

An hour spent in the worship of God is like a cool breeze blowing across a hot and parched earth.

The church is the noblest and best organization in the world. It furnishes the best examples of righteous living, the finest specimens of character, of which the world has any knowledge; exercises the largest influence in the work of reform; promotes honest, progressive, and beneficent government, and more than any other thing makes and maintains the home as a place of virtue, love, righteousness, brotherly kindness, and sacred honor.

Christ gave His best for you. Give Christ your best through His Church.

A nodding congregation may—and may not—mean assent to what the preacher is saying. —*The Baptist*

Here, O my Lord, I see Thee face to face.
　Here would I touch and handle things unseen;
Here taste again the immeasureable grace,
　And all my weariness upon Thee lean.
　　　　　—Horatius Bonar

In following Christ it is the first venture that costs. Once on the way one does not find it harder than other ways. Like the entrance into chilly water, the worst is the plunge. The danger is that one will shrink from the venture, and that everything will be lost for the simple lack of the courage to begin. —J. O. Cresap

Sweet the moments, rich in blessing,
　Which before the cross I spend;
Life and health and peace possessing
　From the sinner's dying Friend.
　　　　　—Walter Shirley

Watch your battery. Your soul is your battery. When you neglect it, it gives no sign. But some day when you sadly need it, it is likely to fail you. Better have it looked after regularly at the service station—the church.

Our church is:
A sanctuary of the Spirit.
A training school for Christian character.
A center of helpful service.
A force for civic righteousness.
A power for God throughout the world.
An unfailing spring of inner refreshment and strength, free to all who come.

To strangers within our gates—We trust that within our church you will find the quiet of the presence of God; the blessed warmth of a real brotherhood; and the abiding truth of the sacred Scriptures.

The Sabbath is the core of our civilization, dedicated to thought and reverence. It invites to the noblest solitude and the noblest society.
—Ralph Waldo Emerson

There have been implanted in man an instinct and a need, which make him discontented till he find content in God. —Hugh Black

"O, for a thousand tongues to sing my great Redeemer's praise:" The fact we do not have a thousand tongues is no excuse for not using the one tongue we do have.

It sounds so much better to say, "Come to church," than "Go to church."

Every one can listen to God.
When men listen, God speaks.
When God speaks, men are changed.
When men are changed, nations change.
—Cecil Rose

We are a nation of open church doors and open Bibles, but open church doors mean nothing if we do not enter, and open Bibles have no value unless they are read and their teachings practiced.

Even if you are too deaf to hear the preacher, the Church is still a good place for listening to God.
—John A. Holmes

No skyscraper can equal the reach of a church spire.

We need the atmosphere of the Christian church for growth in grace. No flower can bloom in a frost.

The church is no more to be blamed for the bad people that are in it than a hospital is to be blamed for the sick people that are in it.
—Elwood S. Falkenstein

It is a big thing to do a small thing well.

To live with Christ, to fill the mind with thoughts of Him, to cleanse the emotions by remembrance of Him, to saturate the spirit with the recollections of His Spirit,—that is the indispensable secret of moral splendor.
—Albert Edward Day

A saint is anyone who makes it easier for us to believe in God.

Too often religion is like soap—those who need it most use it least.

This is the essence of the gospel:
    For God so loved the world,
that He gave His Only
    begotten Son, that whosoever believeth in him
    should not Perish,
    but have Everlasting Life.
—John 3:16

It is the preacher's business to make sinners uncomfortable.

O do not pray for easy lives. Pray to be stronger men. Do not pray for tasks equal to your powers. Pray for powers equal to your task. Then the doing of your work shall be no miracle. But you shall be a miracle. Every day you shall wonder at yourself, at the richness of life which has come to you by the grace of God.
—Phillips Brooks

No man can do more than the will of God, no matter where he goes; no man dare do less than the will of God, no matter where he stays.
—Robert E. Speer

While the church is looking for better methods, God is looking for better men.

Christianity helps us to face the music, even when we don't like the tune.

Church Attendance—The Sabbath—Christian Worship and Work

The man who has not been to church for thirty years is usually the one who says that modern preaching is behind the times.

Religion is like a bank in that neither one pays dividends unless we make deposits.

One hasn't gone far in his Christianity if he frets about Sunday; if the observance of it is irksome to him; if it is a burden, and not wings, a task and not a tool.

Church attendance and worship ought to be identical, but too often they are not.

It is not enough that there should be action in the pulpit—there must be reaction in the pews.
—Calvin Coolidge

Perhaps one can have religion, yet not go to church. But why would anyone who has it want to stay away?

Go to church:
To meet God.
To grow better.
To grow stronger against temptation.
To meet the best people on earth.
To be an example to others.
To be of service to God and man.

I belong to the church because:
If nobody belonged to the church, there would be no church; and if the church with all its influences for good were suddenly taken away, I would want to leave town immediately.
While I may not agree with all its ideas of theology, I do believe in its ideals of life.
While I share in the blessings of a Christian civilization, I want to be square enough to have a share in the church's work.

Joining the church of itself will not save a man's soul, but it saves his life to a useful purpose after his soul is saved.

One of the great needs of the Church is better preaching. Another great need is better listening.

Our Father has a multitude of talkative sons—but the laborers are few.
—*Christian Witness*

All the doors that lead inward to the secret place of the Most High are doors outward—out of self—out of smallness—out of wrong.
—George MacDonald

A Christian is:
A Mind, through which Christ thinks.
A Heart, through which Christ loves.
A Voice, through which Christ speaks.
A Hand, through which Christ lifts.

The person who takes time for prayer usually finds ample time for all the other things needing his attention.

The reason some can't keep the Sabbath holy is because of unholy practices on the other six days of the week.

When Sunday comes, instead of being "all out" for Christ, many of us are "all in."

Go to church to be entertained, and soon you will be forsaking the church to find entertainment elsewhere.

If absence makes the heart grow fonder, how some people must love the church!

Some people treat God like a lawyer. They go to Him only when they are in trouble.

When a church member rests, he rusts.

The way to do a great deal for Christ is to keep on doing a little.

It is surprising how soon some people lose interest in an organization when they lose leadership.

If, before criticizing the sermon, you stop to consider how much it actually cost you, you might conclude that you got your money's worth.
—*The Houghton Line*

Many a church needs the fire of a revival to thaw out its frozen assets.

Religion has no place in your life unless it has first place.

The best way to double a preacher's power is to double his congregation. Try this on him.

As we keep or break the Sabbath, we nobly save or meanly lose the last, best hope by which man rises.
—Abraham Lincoln

"Twenty centuries of history are looking down upon you!"—this was the challenge of Napoleon to his soldiers drawn up before the Egyptian pyramids. When I partake of the Lord's Supper, I feel the challenge not only of Him who gave his life for me, but of the twenty centuries of Christian martyrs who are looking down upon me.   —J. H. Vincent

Freedom of worship should not be interpreted to mean neglect of worship.

Religion is a process continued, not completed.

The Church is a religious home, a sanctuary for worship, a school for religious instruction, a fighting unit for the new world that is building. It is a social center of the highest type, since it gathers into relations of mutual helpfulness people of every age and condition, and since it adds to the attractions of the ordinary club the power of religion and the generous sympathies of the altruistic impulse. The Church is the most broadening and catholic organization among men, since its vision is to the ends of the world whither the gospel is being carried, and since its citizenship is in heaven as well as in the earth.
—Worth M. Tippy

Prayer changes us, not God.

It is a poor preparation for your first Sunday in eternity to have misspent your last Sunday on earth.

Be an on-timer. In time, on time, every time, and all the time, excepting when ahead of time, and that's a little better time.

I find life an exciting business, and it is most exciting when it is lived for others.   —Helen Keller

Fear not to enter His courts in the slenderness of the poor wealth thou canst reckon as thine. Truth in its beauty and love in its tenderness, these are the offerings to lay on His shrine.
—John J. B. Monsell

Chapter III

Patriotism—Citizenship—War and Peace

The public business of the nation is the private business of every citizen.

A good newspaper and Bible in every home, a good schoolhouse in every district, and a church in every neighborhood, all appreciated as they deserve, are the chief support of virtue, morality, civil liberty and religion.
—Benjamin Franklin

I hope that I shall always possess firmness and virtue enough to maintain what I consider the most enviable of all titles, the character of an honest man. —George Washington

If this government itself is ever demoralized it will come from trying to live without work.
—Abraham Lincoln

It is a strange desire that men have, to seek power and lose liberty.
—Francis Bacon

War never determines who is right, only who is left.

You cannot pray for peace with your hands clenched into fists.

If war is hell, it is the church's job to preach against it.

A means to a permanent peace is for all nations to agree not to start another war until the last one is paid for.

South America was settled by the Spanish, who came to that land in search of gold, but North America was settled by the Pilgrim Fathers, who came in search of God. That made a difference.

The ballot is the symbol of citizenship as the flag is the symbol of the country; and like the flag it is worth no more than we make it worth.
—A. R. Wells

The first step in putting religion into politics is putting religion into men.

Living the Golden Rule will bring in the Golden Age.

If there's anything small, or shallow, or ugly about a person, giving him a little authority will bring it out.

The person who can be one thing as well as another in religion or politics usually ends up by being nothing.

It is easy for a person to be zealous for the rights of the minority when he happens to belong to the minority.

The kind of citizens we are is more important than the kind of government we have.

A man can be a citizen of the world without being any the less a citizen of his country.

Too many people are clamoring for freedom to do what ought not to be done.

Too many petty causes get too much loyalty.

No law can change vice into virtue.

If Jesus had had any racial or national prejudice, He could not have been the Saviour for the whole world.

Quick Quotes for Church Bulletins

There are more candidates running for something than there are who stand for something.

The savage tribes, it has been noted, have no taxes to pay. They will have, however, by the time the civilized tribes get through with them.

Let us have faith that right makes might; and in that faith let us, to the end, dare to do our duty as we understand it. —Abraham Lincoln

Unless we can learn the supremacy of spiritual forces, the pallbearers that have carried out other dead civilizations wait at our door.
—Harry Emerson Fosdick

The foundation for religious liberty is laid when a human soul discovers God. —E. Y. Mullins

The truest test of civilization is not the census, nor the size of cities, nor the crops; but the kind of men the country turns out.
—Ralph Waldo Emerson

The human race is divided into two classes—those who go ahead and do something and those who sit still and inquire, "Why wasn't it done the other way?" —Oliver Wendell Holmes

Let every one remember that he who violates the laws of the land tramples on the blood of the fathers and tears asunder the charter of his own and his children's liberty.
—Abraham Lincoln

Militarist—a man who is clamoring for a chance to lay down *your* life for his country.

Before spears can be turned into pruninghooks, hearts of hate must be turned into hearts of love.

Any weakening of the rights of some is a weakening of the rights of all.

The fight for freedom today is, in a real sense, a fight for the idea of brotherhood. . . . The survival of free civilization depends upon the survival of this idea and upon the practical allegiance it commands of all free peoples. —Dwight D. Eisenhower

It costs less to train one hundred children in Christian living than it costs to deal with one average criminal.

There is little use in crying, "Peace, peace," if at the same time we reject the Prince of peace.

There is a lot of injustice in the world, and it isn't all on the other side of the ocean.

Don't vote a straight ticket unless it is filled with straight men.

The peace Christ came to give is not the kind that has to be enforced at the point of a bayonet.

To be honest with the world, one must give it at least the equivalent of what he receives from it.

A statesman is one who looks to the next generation. A politician is one who looks to the next election.

I hope mankind will have reason and sense enough to settle their differences without cutting throats; for in my opinion, there never was a good war or a bad peace.
—Benjamin Franklin

Since wars begin in the minds of men, it is in the minds of men that the defences of peace must be constructed.
—Constitution of The United Nations Educational, Scientific and Cultural Organization

I recognize the sublime truth announced in the Holy Scriptures and proven by all history that those nations only are blest whose God is the Lord. —Abraham Lincoln

The man who is too busy to serve God and humanity is—too busy.
—*Christian Endeavor World*

The rock-ribbed politician usually has a heart of stone.

There are lots of big men in small towns—and vice versa.

For reasons of good citizenship attend church, and there you will find other good reasons for church attendance.

The taxes laid on us by the government are indeed heavy, and if they were the only ones we had to pay, we might more easily discharge them; but we have many others, and much more grievous to some of us. We are taxed twice as much by our idleness, three times as much by our pride, and four times as much by our folly, and from these taxes the commissioners cannot ease or deliver us by allowing an abatement. —Benjamin Franklin

Morality and religion are the two pillars of our society.
—George Washington, Farewell Address

Our fathers have left us a rich spiritual legacy. Surely it is our duty not to squander it but to leave it replenished so that we, in our generation, may bequeath to those who come after us a tradition as noble as was left us.

Many a person has convictions for which he wants someone else to supply the courage.

Some have the courage of their convictions whose convictions don't call for much courage.

No citizen is an asset to himself or his country who seeks to live at the hands of his nation without return.

Patriotism has not discharged its full duty when it hangs out a flag.

A Christian citizen is a man who loves God first, his country next, himself last. He prays when he votes and votes as he prays. In his personal, family, and political life, he unostentatiously sets an example which, if followed by all, would make democracy safe for the world.
—Francis E. Clark

The Church of Jesus Christ is the great balancing power between utter chaos and a world of safety and order.

"I'm up a tree," admitted the bolting Senator, "but my back is against the wall. I'll fight to the last ditch, going down with flags flying and hurling defiance to the foe, soaring on the wings of triumph, regardless of the party lash that barks at my heels." He looked as though he meant it, too.
—*Philadelphia Ledger*

It is a sad fact that many politicians are more concerned with deals than with ideals.

The Lord has as much trouble with soft heads as he has with hard hearts.

All the victor takes over is a heap of rubble, a pile of corpses and a horde of hungry people whose means of existence he has destroyed.
—George Bernard Shaw's comment on atomic warfare

Any person who defrauds the nation by evading customs duties, by shirking public tasks, by falsely representing his liabilities to taxes, or by rendering less than market value in every transaction with the government, is something else—and less—than a patriot.

Civilization requires that the caliber of guns be made smaller and the caliber of men greater.

The Church has the only cure for social ills. It alone deals with the disease—sin—rather than with symptoms.

He that would govern others must first be lord of himself, and he only is lord of himself who is consciously and habitually the servant of God.
—Alexander Maclaren

Your ballot is your birthright as an American citizen. Do not despise it.

The mounds of Babylon, the ruins of Palmyra, and Baalbek, the broken columns of the Roman Forum, all utter louder than Sinai the same warning. No matter how intellectual a people may become, how far the reach of its power, it seems to be an irresistible law that the nation that forgets God is wiped off the face of the earth.
—R. J. Cooke

The salvation of America will lie in a general return to the old-fashioned, commonplace, everyday virtues that make sterling character, and which we are surrendering to the brilliant and the spectacular. Honesty, courage, purity and self-control are far more needed today than any career of glory or any exploits that win the plaudits of the galleries.—*Examiner*

After a war, it takes longer to settle up than to settle down.

The world can't be cleaned up with soft soap.

The old-fashioned sermon on hell wasn't so different from the ones you hear today on current events.

Just a little horse sense would mean a stable government.

The man without a country is no worse off than a man without a church.

"In God We Trust" on our coins means nothing unless in God we trust.

Next to the sin of voting wrongly is the sin of not voting at all.
—Theodore L. Cuyler

Let us impart the blessings we possess to the whole family of mankind.
—George Washington

History is littered with the stories of nations destroyed by their own wealth. —Calvin Coolidge

Voting ought to be done as reverently as praying.

The one safe principle at the polls is the will of God. What will most glorify Him? —Robert E. Speer

True patriotism acknowledges the law of God in national affairs. It is not by accident that our coins tell the world: "In God We Trust."

You may fool all the people some of the time; you can even fool some of the people all the time; but you can't fool all of the people all the time.
—Abraham Lincoln

War is a loaded pistol aimed at the heart of civilization itself, with a hair-trigger held by an unsteady hand.
—Newton D. Baker

I am not bound to win, but I am bound to be true. I am not bound to succeed, but I am bound to live up to what light I have.
—Abraham Lincoln

Righteousness exalteth a nation, but sin is a reproach to any people.
—Inscription over the pulpit in the chapel at West Point

The best reformers the world has ever had are those who began with themselves.

Some people lose their liberty by taking too many liberties.

To seek peace, to make peace, or to keep peace we need peacemakers, men and women, under God's control, at peace within themselves, a fellowship rising above the barriers of race and nation, an army of life-changers, demonstrating the friendship of the new world order. —Stephen Foot

Don't make the mistake of thinking you are great just because you possess some great man's weakness.

Democracy is based upon the conviction that there are extraordinary possibilities in ordinary people.
—Harry Emerson Fosdick

The time has come to stop this silly un-American saber rattling, and get down to the task of laying the foundations of a peaceful world.
—Robert M. Hutchins

PATRIOTISM—CITIZENSHIP—WAR AND PEACE

The little sins of great men are often responsible for the great sins of little men. —John Timothy Stone

The greatest danger to free speech is that many who have it are too free with it.

I had rather be defeated in a cause that will ultimately triumph, than triumph in a cause that will ultimately be defeated. —Woodrow Wilson

The only way out is up.

The grace of God still enables men to live straight in a crooked world.

The world is getting better. The people sent to jail are a much higher class than formerly.—*Canton Repository*

It's hard to dislike a chap who likes you, isn't it? Well, there's your peace plan. —*Stockton Independent*

There are no war-like peoples, just war-like leaders.—Ralph J. Bunche

America is great because she is good, and if America ever ceases to be good, she will cease to be great.
—Dwight D. Eisenhower

Statesmanship is seeing where almighty God is going and then getting things out of His way.
—Frank Gunsaulus

What is liberty without wisdom and without virtue? It is the greatest of all possible evils: for it is folly, vice, and madness, without tuition or restraint.
—Burke, *Reflection on the French Revolution*

The men we take days off to honor, seldom took days off.

Inscription on the Statue of Liberty:
Give me your tired, your poor,
Your huddled masses yearning to breathe free,
The wretched refuse of your teeming shore,
Send these, the homeless, tempest-tost to me,
I lift my lamp beside the golden door.
—Emma Lazarus

What this country needs more than anything else is fewer people telling this country what it needs more than anything else.

There is no greater sign of a general decay of virtue in a nation, than a want of zeal in its inhabitants for the good of their country.
—Joseph Addison

When men are good, government cannot be bad.

Men must be governed by God, or they will be ruled by tyrants.
—William Penn

Only the weakness of good men gives evil men their power.

That patriotism is purest that disregards opportunities for personal honor, and falters not when called to do the difficult duty, though it must be done in obscurity, far from the blaze of public approval. Patriotism burns brightest in the unselfish heart.

Justice is as strictly due between neighbor nations as between neighbor citizens. A highwayman is as much a robber when he plunders in a gang, as when single; and a nation that makes an unjust war is only a *great gang*. —Benjamin Franklin

When the state is most corrupt, then laws are most multiplied.—Tacitus

The less people speak of their greatness, the more we think of it.
—Francis Bacon

We must not in the course of public life expect immediate approbation, and immediate grateful acknowledgment of our services. But let us persevere through abuse and even injury. The internal satisfaction of a good conscience is always present, and time will do us justice in the minds of the people, even of those at present most prejudiced against us.
—Benjamin **Franklin**

Sometimes people call me an idealist. Well, that is the way I know that I am an American. America is the only idealistic nation in the world.
—Woodrow Wilson

Our country hath a gospel of her own to preach and practice before all the world; the freedom and divinity of man, the glorious claims of human brotherhood, and the soul's fealty to none but God.
—James Russell Lowell

The strength of a democracy is judged by the quality of the services rendered by its citizens. —Plato

Man's capacity for justice makes democracy possible; but man's inclination to injustice makes democracy necessary. —Reinhold Niebuhr

Standing as I do in view of God and eternity I realize that patriotism is not enough. I must have no hatred or bitterness for anyone.
—Edith Cavell

Chapter IV

Children and Youth

Children are God's apostles, day by day sent forth to preach of love and hope and peace.
—James Russell Lowell

Time marches on:
Charming Childhood,
Tender Teens,
Teachable Twenties,
Tireless Thirties,
Fiery Forties,
Forceful Fifties,
Serious Sixties,
Sober Seventies,
Aching Eighties,
Death, the Sod, God.
—Author Unknown

Those who presume to teach the "young idea how to shoot" should know at what to aim.

Often the best way to correct your children is to correct the example you are setting for them.

I have often thought what a melancholy world this would be without children; and what an inhuman world without the aged.
—Samuel Taylor Coleridge

The perpetuity of this nation depends upon the religious education of the young. —George Washington

In our discussions of the religious needs of young people we are tempted to regard Christianity as a religion of the old, which has by some means or other to be adapted to the minds of the young. I think we should be nearer the truth if we were to regard it as originally a religion of the young which has lost some of its savor by being adapted to the minds of the old.
—L. P. Jacks

In the days when a wood shed stood behind the American home, a great deal of what now passes as juvenile delinquency was settled out of court.
—Link

The need of the hour is not for parents who send their children to Sunday school and church, but for parents who say, "Come on, let's go."

If you want to stay young, associate with young people; if you want to feel your age, try to keep up with them.

In the little world where children have their existence, there is nothing so finely perceived and so keenly felt as injustice.   —Charles Dickens

I once heard somebody say that you can't tell whether a parent has been a success or a failure until you find out what happens to the grandchildren.
—Richard L. Strout

God has His small interpreters; the child must teach the man.
John G. Whittier

Whoso loves a child loves not himself but God; whoso delights a child labors with God in His workshop of the world of hearts; whoso helps a child brings the Kingdom of God; whoso saves a child from the fingers of evil sits in the seat with the builders of cities and the procurers of peace.
—Norman Duncan

Many parents need a good spanking.

The youth who does not look up, will look down; and the spirit that does not soar is destined perhaps to grovel.   —Benjamin Disraeli

Quick Quotes for Church Bulletins

Children need models more than critics.

A boy is a young person who shouldn't do the things his father did at that age.

At fourteen William Shakespeare began his career. At thirteen Longfellow wrote his first poem. Robert Browning produced his "Paracelsus" while yet in his teens. At seventeen Alexander Hamilton launched his career as a statesman. "The Raven" was written by Edgar Allan Poe at twenty-four. Alexander the Great had conquered the world at twenty-three, and Columbus was twenty-eight when he announced his plans to find India. John Smith staked out a colonial empire in Virginia at twenty-seven. Martin Luther started the Reformation at thirty, and John Calvin, founder of the Presbyterian Church, entered the pastorate at seventeen. Spurgeon at twenty was pastor of London Tabernacle. Francis E. Clark was in his twenties when he founded Christian Endeavor. Joan of Arc was an all-time heroine at nineteen. Patrick Henry cried, "Give me liberty, or give me death" at twenty-seven. Jesus was thirty when He preached "The Sermon on the Mount," and soon thereafter, with His pierced hands, lifted the Roman Empire off its hinges.

Call not that man wretched who, whatever ills he suffers, has a child to love. —Robert Southey

A torn jacket is soon mended, but hard words bruise the heart of a child.
—Henry W. Longfellow

The attitude of mind of some parents is humorously revealed in the command of a mother who said: "Johnny, run upstairs and see what your little brother is doing, and tell him not to."

Socrates once said, "Could I climb to the highest place in Athens, I would lift my voice and proclaim—Fellow-citizens, why do you turn and scrape every stone to gather wealth, and take so little care of your children to whom one day you must relinquish it all?"
—*Family Circle*

Another explanation of the modern child's manners is that too many woodsheds have been converted into garages.
—Associated Editors, Chicago

Riddle: Which adds up to more, 10+60, or 60+10? Answer: If a child of ten becomes a Christian, it is better than if he should become a Christian at sixty. It doesn't require a brilliant intellect to figure this out.

If you wish success in life make Perseverance your bosom friend, Experience your wise teacher, Caution your elder brother, and Hope your guardian genius. —Joseph Addison

If we had paid no more attention to our plants than we have to our children, we would now be living in a jungle of weeds. —Luther Burbank

When a young person gets his first glimpse at the literal truth of Christ's paradoxical axiom, "He that loseth his life for my sake shall find it," he has taken the first step away from the dark prison of his heathen self into a Christian realization of his oneness with his fellow-man.
—Dorothy Canfield Fisher

Jesus lifted childhood up and set it in the midst. If the patter of little feet on the stairs and the sound of little voices in the house are music to us, and if the pressure of little fingers and the touches of little lips can make us thrill with gratitude and prayer, we owe this sunshine to Jesus Christ.
—James Stalker

The most influential of all educational factors is the conversation in a child's home. —William Temple

48

Chapter V

Christian Education

There can be no final disharmony between thought and things, between faith and knowledge, between science and religion. If there is any apparent disharmony it must either be our knowledge that is wrong or our faith that is not deep and pure enough.
—John A. Hutton

There is nothing so costly as ignorance. —Horace Mann

A college education never hurt anyone who was willing to learn something afterward.
—*Sunshine Magazine*

It is well to remember that open-mindedness is not the same as empty-mindedness.

The feelings are to be disciplined, the passions are to be restrained; true and worthy motives are to be inspired; a profound religious feeling is to be instilled, and pure morality inculcated under all circumstances. All this is comprised in education.
—Daniel Webster

Wisdom is knowing what to do; skill is knowing how to do it; virtue is in doing it well.

He is best educated who is most useful. —Elbert Hubbard

A "highbrow" is an ordinary man educated beyond his intelligence.

While it is true that religion needs learning, it is true that learning needs religion. —B. H. Branscomb

There is need for one to grow down as well as up. —M. E. Dodd

It is said that Thomas A. Edison welcomed deafness because of the freedom it gave him to think his own thoughts.

Getting educated is one thing; keeping educated is another.

Good teaching causes scholars to think, to do, to be.

Some ignorance is amusing, some is amazing, and some is appalling.

'Tis education forms the common mind:
Just as the twig is bent the tree's inclined.
—Alexander Pope

Character is the joint product of nature and nurture.

Religion is the mother, the church the nursery of religion.

The best remedy for conceit is to sit down and make a list of all the things you don't know.

There is one thing stronger than armies, and that is an idea whose time has come. —Victor Hugo

There is nothing so strong or safe in an emergency of life as the simple truth. —Charles Dickens

If a man empties his purse into his head, no man can take it away from him; an investment in knowledge always pays the best interest.
—Benjamin Franklin

What sculpture is to a block of marble, education is to the soul.
—Joseph Addison

It is better to understand a little than to misunderstand a lot.
—Anatole France

Adult education too often is confused with adulterated education.

To know what to do with what you know is the essence of true wisdom.

It is an evidence of mediocrity to have settled opinions on unsettled subjects.

Pretending to be wise is what makes some people appear so foolish.

The test of true education is whether it causes us to do the thing we have to do, when it ought to be done, whether we like it or not.
—Author Unknown

The happiness of your life depends upon the quality of your thoughts.
—Marcus Antoninus

He who has truth in his heart need never fear the want of persuasion on his tongue. —John Ruskin

I say the acknowledgment of God in Christ, accepted by thy reason, solves for thee all questions in the earth and out of it.
—Robert Browning

The most dangerous of all false doctrines is the one seasoned with a little truth.

If we work on marble, it will perish. If we work on brass, time will efface it. If we rear temples, time will crumble them into dust. But if we work on immortal minds; if we imbue them with principles, with the just fear of God and love of our fellow men, we engrave on those tablets something which will brighten all eternity.
—Daniel Webster

The brand of ignorance that destroys the soul is knowing so much that is not so.

You don't have to be listed in *Who's Who* to know what's what.

When a new idea occupies a vacant mind, it has a glorious time.

A man who doesn't know how to learn from his mistakes turns the best schoolmaster out of his life.
—Henry Ward Beecher

To educate a man in mind and not in morals is to educate a menace to society. —Theodore Roosevelt

The human creature needs first of all to be educated, not that he may speak, but that he may have something to say. —Thomas Carlyle

An intelligent man gives up his childish notions of science and philosophy, but does not give up science or philosophy. So he outgrows his childish notions of religion, but holds on to his religion.

One is old only when he allows his mind to become a mausoleum for the storage of dead ideas.

Light is truth. Be a light seeker. Truth is ever ahead, not behind. Keep pursuing it.

The true measure of the worth of education lies not in what you can get from the world, but in what you can give to it.

In the dark ages, people belonged to kings. When the light of education spread, kings belonged to the people.

Seventy roosters recently came across the ocean with an insurance policy of $250,000 on them. They were educated roosters, trained for vaudeville stunts. Had they been ordinary roosters, their value probably would have been about $2 each, and they wouldn't have got far from home. It pays to get an education.

The business of the church is to produce Christlike character and equip for Christlike service.

The real test of the educational program of a church lies not in the ability of a catechumen to answer all the questions in the catechism, nor in the ability of children to recite many scripture verses from memory, but in how much Christlike character has been developed.

Contempt for an uneducated person is no mark of an education.

For some reason, the emptier the head the less it takes to fill it.

Honestly, now, could you pass an entrance examination for heaven today?

The mechanic that would perfect his work must first sharpen his tools.
—Confucius

No man can be called friendless when he has God and the companionship of good books.
—Elizabeth Barrett Browning

"Come now, and let us reason together." The Church is the divinely created custodian of God's teachings in the world.

Teaching is not a flow of words, nor the draining of an hour glass, but an effectual procuring that a man comes to know something he knew not before, or to know it better.
—Robert South

A wise man is like a pin. His head keeps him from going too far.

The past is like a bank where an unlimited number of ideas have been deposited to our credit.
—Lynn Harold Hough

If the battle of civilization is lost in the schools, who is going to win it afterwards? If the whole community is set wrong in its education, what chances have the clergy of being able to set it right from the pulpit? To begin by starting the community on the wrong road, in the plastic period, and then, when it is grown up, to send out the parson and the policeman to bring it back—what fool's enterprise could compare with that?
—L. P. Jacks

It is a great thing to kindle men's thoughts and lift them upward, to interpret the world as God has made it, to invoke the latent powers of the soul that men may rise from their bondage at the touch of a living Saviour. It is a great thing to inspire men; and only he can inspire who is himself inspired.

The fear of the Lord is the beginning of wisdom. —Proverbs 9:10

Twelve things to learn:
The value of time
The need of perseverence
The pleasure of serving
The dignity of simplicity
The true worth of character
The power of kindness
The influence of example
The obligation of duty
The wisdom of economy
The virtue of patience
The nobility of labor
The teachings of Him who said, "Learn of me."

Look for the man whose "education" is finished. He is apt to know too many things that the world is trying to leave behind.
—*Western Christian Advocate*

You would not accept a prescription for a medicine from a bootblack. Why accept advice on spiritual matters from those not prepared to give it?

The University of the People is the Sunday School.
—David Lloyd George

The aims of Christian Education:
A body strong and supple
An intellect able to think
A heart of love
A conscience for righteousness
Appreciation of the beautiful
A strong will to choose the right

Learn as though you were to live forever; live as though you were to die tomorrow.

No man can be wholly uneducated who really knows the Bible, nor can

any man be considered truly educated who is ignorant of it.
—Schurman

He who will not be ruled by the rudder, must be ruled by the rock.
—Isaac D'Israeli

Wisdom is knowing what to do; skill is knowing how to do it; virtue lies in doing it, and doing it well.
—David Storr Jordan

We spend more for chewing gum than for books. It is much easier to exercise the chin than the mind.
—*Eastern Methodist*

Always remember, a man is not rewarded for having brains, but for using them.

When I was fourteen, I thought my father was an old ignoramus. When I became twenty-one I was surprised at how much he had learned in seven years. —Mark Twain

The class yell of the school of experience is, *"Ouch!"*

The only apologetic for Jesus' teaching that I find in any way reasonable is the one which Jesus Himself propounded—experience. His way of life is not to be followed merely because He recommended it, or because He was virgin-born, or was a part of the Godhead, or could work miracles, or for any other reason than that experience will prove that it is a good way, none better, if one have but the understanding and tenacity of purpose to cleave to it.
—Albert Jay Nock

A man's greatness is measured by his kindness; his education and intellect by his modesty. His ignorance is betrayed by his suspicions and prejudices, and his real caliber is measured by the consideration and tolerance he has for others.
—William J. H. Boetcker

Do not suppose that Wisdom is so much flattered at having you for a pupil that she will set you easy lessons, and yet give you a gold medal.
—T. T. Lynch

If His Word once teach us, shoot a ray
Through all the heart's dark chambers and reveal
Truths undiscerned but by that holy light,
Then all is plain.
—William Cowper

A handful of good life is worth a bushel of learning.
—C. H. Spurgeon

Chapter VI

The Stewardship of Money

Nothing is ours to keep for ourselves. Money, talent, time, whatever it may be that we possess, is only ours to use. This is the great law written everywhere. No one owns anything for himself alone, and no one can live to himself alone.
—*Presbyterian Advance*

Blessed is the man who loves the Lord with his pocketbook as well as with his heart.

It is good to have money, and the things that money can buy, but it is good, too, to check up once in a while and make sure you haven't lost the things money can't buy.
—George H. Lorimer

Fewer men survive the test of prosperity than the pressure of poverty.

Personal religion also means purse-and-all religion.

Deeper giving means deeper living.

Do good with what thou hast, or it will do thee no good.

The church suffers sometimes by trying to do things with money that can be done only by human hearts and hands.

Money is an article which may be used as a universal passport to everything except Heaven, and as a universal provider of everything except happiness.
—*Wall Street Journal*

I know a lot of millionaires, but only a few of them ever smile.
—Andrew Carnegie

God is more concerned about *you* than about *yours*.

If we belong to Christ, it follows logically that everything we have belongs to Him.

The Lord loveth a cheerful giver—also a grateful receiver.

Each generation makes some transforming discovery in God's Book; what is "stewardship" but God's word for this generation?

Stewardship puts the Golden Rule in business in place of the rule of gold.

When a man gets rich, God gets a partner or the man loses his soul.

A selfish "Christian" is something else—and less—than Christian.

Money-raising devices are crutches on which a church may hobble along; stewardship-giving enables a church to "run and not grow weary."
—*Stewardship Nuggets*

Once there was a congregation that was so penurious that when the preacher asked them to sing "Old Hundred," they sang instead "The Ninety and Nine." They thought it saved one per cent.

Don't censure the Ladies' Aid Society, which gives all it makes, if you don't even give the tithe.

A man is never so on trial as in the moment of excessive good fortune.
—Lew Wallace

If your treasure is on earth, you are going from it; if it is in heaven, you are going to it.

It's easy to know when to stop giving to the Lord's work. Just give till the Master stops giving to you.

When we place our contribution on the collection plate, we are not giving to the Lord; we are just taking our hands off what belongs to Him.

A ministerial brother says the word "parishioner" should be spelled "pay-rishioner."

It takes grace, grit, and greenbacks to run a church and carry on the work of the Kingdom of God.
—*Lutheran Messenger*

It has been said there are five times as many verses of scripture in the New Testament that have to do with some phase of stewardship than there are verses dealing with the subject of prayer. One has to wonder what would happen to the average pastor if he preached five times as much about money as about prayer.

Giving is one of the graces of the Christian life, not a burden.

Some people conduct their lives on the cafeteria plan—self-service only.

It takes more ingenuity to spend money wisely than to earn it.

Seeking empties a life; giving fills it.

Give not from the top of your purse, but from the bottom of your heart.

When you give till it hurts, it makes you feel good.

Judas was the original charter member of the "Look Out for No. 1 Club."

A man may give without loving, but he cannot love without giving.

When we take the first "r" out of prayers, we help answer them.

It costs to follow Jesus Christ, but it costs more not to.

Tithing also means that a man gets nine dollars from God for every dollar God gets from the man.

As the love of money is the root of all kinds of evil, so the love of what money can do is a root of all kinds of righteousness, peace, and good will in the world.

Just pretending to be rich is what keeps some people poor.

Do what you can, where you are, with what you have.

Too many people apply the principles of "saving grace" to their pocketbooks, rather than to their souls.

The measure of an individual's spiritual condition lies in his willingness and desire to give and share.

Stewardship puts the budge in budget. —*Stewardship Nuggets*

A dollar won't do as much as it once did. But we won't do as much for a dollar as we once did either.
—Ben Sallows, Alliance, Nebraska, *Times-Herald*

In this world it is not what we give up, but what we take up, that makes us rich. —Henry Ward Beecher

The giving of money is one of the outward and visible signs of the right spirit moving inwardly in the hearts of the people who give it.

Life is measured not by accumulation but by outlay; not by how much saved, but by how much expended; not by distance traveled, but by the road taken.

Clouds give rain; flowers give scent; the sun gives light and warmth; the bees give honey; the cows give milk; and the Church is in the world to give it Christ.

The lad who gave his loaves and fishes didn't have to go without his dinner.

Only when the greatness of one's soul exceeds the greatness of one's possessions will great possessions be safe in his hands.

Money talks, but its owner must be its interpreter.

Wealth is a good servant, but a very bad master. —Francis Bacon

One of the standing miracles of the Christian religion is its record of achievements with small resources.

More money in your purse means greater obligation to God and man.

Use the talents you have, and you will not feel so keenly your need of more talents.

You must possess your things or they will possess you.

The Church needs today:
More tithes and fewer drives;
More action and less faction;
More workers and fewer shirkers;
More backers and fewer slackers;
More praying and less straying;
More burdenbearers and fewer talebearers.

No man is so poor as he who has nothing but money.

Stewardship is the recognition of God's claim upon both your purse and your person.

If your riches are yours, why don't you take them with you to the other world? —Benjamin Franklin

Promises to God should be considered as binding as those you make at a bank.

Some folks give according to their means, and some according to their meanness. —George Eliot

If everybody cared enough, and everybody shared enough, for everybody there would be enough.

God wants the offerer more than He wants the offering.

Selfishness with much can do little; love with little can do much.

In the sight of God, the size of your gift is determined by what you have left.

Jesus teaches that a man's attitude to the Kingdom of God is revealed by his attitude to his property.

Money is the stored-up energy of human toil and can be converted again into action in the work of many men. It can stretch out its arms of power around the world, and send light to the most remote and destitute.
—Sherwood Eddy

When one gives himself to Christ, the giving of all lesser things becomes easy.

Dollars and sense should go together.

It is love that gives value to every other gift: love is the currency of faith in truth, the instrument of the Christian business.

Some folks don't let the right hand know what the left hand is doing because they don't want to embarrass the right hand.

"When I look at the congregation," said a preacher, "I ask, where are the poor? When I look at the collection, I ask, where are the rich?"

It requires a strong constitution to withstand repeated attacks of prosperity.

It was said of a certain man, he would not cast his bread upon the water until he was sure it would come back a seven-layer cake.

A penny will hide the biggest star in the universe, if you hold it close enough to your eye.

All you can hold in your cold, dead hand is what you have given away.
—Joaquin Miller

We witness by that for which we give; by what we give; by the way we give.

Do you possess your money? Or does your money possess you?

Generous giving means noble living.

Contentment consists not in great wealth, but in few wants.
—Epictetus

The Kingdom of God cannot be built of left-overs.

There is a difference between making a good living, and living a good life.

To complain that life has no joys while there is a single creature whom we may relieve by our bounty, assist by our counsels, or enliven by our presence, is to lament the loss of that which we possess, and is just as rational as to die of thirst with the cup in our hands. —Fitzosborne

If God had access to more hearts that are cushioned in wealth, other hearts that are stretched on the spiked bed of poverty would find a respite from sorrow and pain.
—Albert E. Day

God cannot assume responsibility for our lives unless we are willing for Him to control our spending and our buying. That involves not mere tithing, setting aside one-tenth of our income for religious uses, though that is a good beginning. It involves the stewardship of ten-tenths of our income. —Albert E. Day

Mammon is the largest slave-holder in the world. —Frederic Saunders

If you make money your god, it will plague you like the devil.
—Henry Fielding

To turn all we possess into the channels of universal love becomes the business of our lives.
—John Woolman

Christians sometimes feel that when prosperity favors them, Satan is leaving them alone and God is blessing them. It may be vice versa.

Chapter VII

Missions and Evangelism

A missionary diet cures the ills of many a church.

There is a mighty *"go"* in the word *"go*spel."

Christianity is ours because missionaries once came to us.

I have but one candle to burn, and would rather burn it out where people are dying in darkness, than in a land which is flooded with light.
—A Missionary

God had an only Son, and He was a missionary.

In fishing for men there is no closed season.

Personal workers get better results when they approach sinners with tears in their eyes rather than with arguments on their lips.

It isn't difficult to get people to serve on the "Lookout" Committee; our difficulty is to get personnel for the "Go-out" Committee.

When the church stops seeking the lost, it is lost.

If more "saints" would heed the admonition to "go," more sinners would accept the invitation to "come."

Confidential question: Is anybody in church this morning because you asked him to come?

The near-sighted woman who talked religion to a wooden Indian in front of a cigar store later declared she would rather be a live Christian and talk religion to a wooden Indian, than a wooden Christian who never talked religion to anybody.
—*Christian Herald Almanac*

Have you ever felt the joy of winning a soul to Christ? I tell you there is no joy this side of heaven which excels it—the grasp of the hand of one who says, "By your means I was turned from darkness to light."
—C. H. Spurgeon

Jesus was deeply concerned over three classes of people—the least, the lost, and the last.

Christ gave His disciples a program, and the power to carry it out.

Nothing makes one feel so strong as a call for help.
—George MacDonald

The only Christianity that can do anything for us is a Christianity that makes us want to do something for others. —John McDowell

The missionary enterprise is not the church's afterthought. It is the church's forethought. It is not secondary and optional, it is primary and vital. —John McDowell

Christ alone can save the world, but Christ cannot save the world alone.

There is no evidence that the intellectual capacities of one race are superior to those of any other.
—Caroline Singer

Christ made evangelism primary, and what Christ made primary the church dare not consider secondary.

There is need for evangelism as long as there is an unsaved soul in the community.

We live in a world in which the *vast* majority of our fellow men eat too little, live too wretchedly, and die too young.   —Warren G. Austin

What the world has been waiting for through the centuries is a sample Christian nation. America has the best chance of being that sample. Consequently every movement which expresses Christian ideals in American life makes easier the task of the missionary abroad. On the other hand, any custom that is unjust makes more difficult the foreign worker's task.
—Edward Laird Mills

It costs less to send missionaries to foreign countries than it does to send soldiers—and it's a lot safer for the rest of us.

One place where prayer fails is in expecting God to do things for us which He can only do through us.

It has been said that at least one half of the people of the world have never worn shoes.

Christ calls:
"Come unto me!"
"Take my yoke!"
"Learn of me!"
"Go ye!"

Too many just talk brotherhood, leaving it to the missionary to exemplify it.

People ask, "Who *was* Buddha? Who *was* Napoleon?" But always, "Who *is* Jesus Christ?" Jesus is not a memory, a historical character; he lives and works today.

Every Christian witness in this tight-knit world today is a Christian witness everywhere. —Emory Ross

The Kingdom of Heaven is not only a gift; it is a task.
—E. Stanley Jones

At a missionary meeting, when contributions for the great cause were asked for, the plates were heaped with coins and bank notes. Among them, however, was a card on which a young man had written, "Myself," and had signed his name. He had given more than all the rest.

God helps those who help others rather than themselves.

Science has made this world a neighborhood; the Church must make it a brotherhood.

You can win more friends in two months by becoming interested in other people than you can win in two years by trying to get other people interested in you. —Dale Carnegie

The Church that, in its passion for others forgets itself will, in that forgetfulness, find itself.
—W. H. P. Faunce

Kindness has converted more sinners than either zeal, eloquence or learning.   —F. W. Faber

It is better to light a candle than to curse the darkness.—Old Proverb

There is not enough darkness in all the world to put out the light of one small candle.   —Author Unknown

When God asks you questions concerning your duty to the unsaved, do you answer them in your own favor, or in His and theirs?

The Spirit of God can convert the unsaved, but He needs Spirit-filled Christians as exhibits to prove His saving power.

The fact that you do not live up to the light you have is proof that the heathen cannot live up to their light.

Many of the true heroes of the world are not athletic, have never seen battle's carnage, nor have been to Hollywood. They have been too busy plodding away on mission fields.

Jesus is the Way. Have you ever led one soul into that Way?

Missionaries to a barbarous people deserve a vote of thanks from the commercial world.—Robert Moffatt

If you want to follow Jesus Christ, you must follow him to the ends of the earth; for that is where he is going. —Robert E. Speer

"My business," said William Carey, "is to extend the Kingdom of God. I only cobble shoes to pay expenses."

Chapter VIII

The Holy Bible

If you know the Author, you will love His Book.

The Bible needs less defense and more practice.

To know the Bible is to love it; to love it is to accept it; to accept it means life eternal.
—Willard L. Johnson

The Bible. When the days are dark, men need its light. When the times are hard, men need its comfort. When the outlook is discouraging, men need its confidence. When despair is abroad, men need its word of hope.
—Robert E. Speer

The best thing men can do is to spread the Bible and to get it read and obeyed. This would be the end of hard times, of poverty, of unemployment, of injustice, of wrong, of war.
—Robert E. Speer

Some people thank God for the open Bible who never bother to open it.

The Bible is not only the world's best seller; it is man's best purchase.

There is no danger of leaving the Bible behind; at least not until we catch up with it.

If there is dust on your Bible, don't call it holy dust.

No one is saved by buying a Bible he does not read; and no one is saved by reading a Bible he does not obey.

To master the Bible, the Bible must first master you.

Some books are for our information; some for our inspiration; the Bible is for our transformation.

Of one thing I am convinced, do what we will, oppose it as we may, it is the Christian Bible that will sooner or later work out the regeneration of our land.
—The Maharajah of Travancore

The Bible has called into existence tens of thousands of other books.
—Henry van Dyke

The Bible, the ancient book, which seemed to bind us to an outworn past, has become our charter of liberty.
—E. F. Scott

The gospel of Jesus Christ is not only a gospel for all men, but it is a gospel for the whole man.

We can never break God's laws; we can only break ourselves against them.
—George Adam Smith

What to read:
If you are "all out of sorts" read Hebrews 12.
If you are losing confidence in men, read I Corinthians 13.
If you have the blues, read Psalm 27.
If your pocketbook is empty, read Psalm 37.
If people seem unkind, read John 15.
If you are discouraged about your work, read Psalm 126.
If you cannot have your own way, read James 3.

What to do with your Bible:
Know it in the head;
Stow it in the heart;
Show it in the life;

The Holy Bible

Sow it in the world;
Read it to be wise;
Believe it to be safe;
Practice it to be holy.

Your Bible:
Dig it up,
Write it down,
Pray it in,
Live it out,
Pass it on.

The things men live by are found in the Word of God. In its pages men have found help for their deepest needs, comfort for their shattered spirits, light for their darkest hours.

Always the Bible has inspired the noblest courage and the most sublime actions of man. Heroes have dedicated their lives to its principles. Martyrs have died with its words on their lips.

The Bible is the support of the strong and the consolation of the weak; the dependence of organized government and the foundation of religion. —Calvin Coolidge

In that humble log cabin which was the Lincoln home they tell us that at one time there was but a single book, but it was the Book. With Almighty God for a schoolmaster and His Book for a text, no wonder that scholar shook the world. —John A. Shedd

What the Bible does not say, it suggests.

Holy Scripture is set as a kind of lantern for us in the night of this present life. —Gregory the Great

Voltaire boasted his work would make the Bible extinct in 100 years. Recently his 92 volumes sold for $2.00. —*Rural Churchman*

The Bible, as no other book, will lift our vision from the murky flats of life's low levels to the sunlit summits of faith and prayer. —George H. Ferris

Just as a road map has little value when used as a tablecloth, but is indispensable when we take a trip in unfamiliar territory, so our Bibles are valueless as shelf ornaments, but priceless as guides to daily religious living.

If we abide by the principles taught in the Bible, our country will go on prospering and to prosper; but if we and our posterity neglect its instructions and authority, no man can tell how sudden a catastrophe may overwhelm us and bury our glory in profound obscurity. —Daniel Webster

The Bible is a book in comparison with which all others in my eyes are of minor importance, and which in all my perplexities and distresses has never failed to give me light and strength. —Robert E. Lee

The Bible is the great book of origins and destiny. It alone deals authoritatively with the two supreme questions, *Whence* and *whither*. —American Bible Society

We are living in a confusion of tongues; many men are offering many contradictory solutions of the world's ills. We need to hear God speak. And the Bible gives us God's voice, in His own words, with His own divine and infallible solution for the world's ills as no other book ever possessed by men.
—American Bible Society

The gospel is the fulfillment of all hopes, the perfection of all philosophy, the interpretation of all revelation, the key to all the seeming contradictions of the physical and moral world. —Max Muller

Believe me, sir, never a night goes by, be I ever so tired, but I read the Word of God before I go to bed. —Douglas MacArthur

Not simply His coming and His going, not simply His birth, or death, but the living, total life of Jesus is the world's salvation. And the Book in which His life shines orbed and distinct is the world's treasure. —Phillips Brooks

Dust on your Bible is not evidence it is a dry Book.

What would we think of any man who, in studying some great masterpiece of art, concentrated his entire attention upon what looked to him like a fly-speck in the corner? A large proportion of the much wanted "critical study of the Bible" is a laborious and scholarly investigation of supposed fly-specks. —R. A. Torrey

It isn't the style of the Bible that makes it unpopular with moderns, but the fact that it cramps their style.
—*Pasadena Evening Post*

The great question is not what you make of the Bible, but what the Bible makes of you.

Chapter IX

Temperance

"Beverage alcohol," said a doctor who knew whereof he spoke, "gives you a red nose, a black eye, a white liver, a yellow streak, a green brain, a dark brown breath, and a blue outlook."

There is no such thing as moderation in the use of alcoholic liquor. He who drinks a little drinks too much.

It is not merely the trail of the serpent that must be gotten rid of, but the serpent that makes the trail.

Anything that mars or weakens human personality is sin.

Secrets are not preserved well in alcohol.

There is not a thought in a hogshead of beer; there is not an idea in a whole brewery. It stupefies without invigorating, and its effect upon the brain is to stagnate thought.
—Theodore Roosevelt, quoted in *Epworth Herald*

No one wants any drinking man to be at the mercy of machinery and no one wants to be at the mercy of machinery in the hands of a drinking man.   —Henry Ford

Alcoholism is a disease, but it can be cured by the Great Physician.

Making a sin legal does not make it harmless.

Liquor and liquidation! There is a close connection between the two.

The "wets" fight prohibition, not because it doesn't prohibit, as they claim, but because it does.

Whiskey has many defenders, but no defense.   —Abraham Lincoln

Drink has broken up more homes and wrecked more lives than any other cause.   —James Cardinal Gibbons

The worst of all delusions is to think a nation can drink itself into prosperity.

Whereas, the use of intoxicating liquors as a beverage is productive of pauperism, degeneration, and crime, and believing that it is our duty to discourage that which produces more evil than good, we therefore pledge ourselves to abstain from the use of intoxicating liquors as a beverage.
—Pledge written and signed by Abraham Lincoln

The person who believes it is right to sell intoxicants surely can't believe that anything is wrong.

The man who drinks and then drives is likely to get the *quart* before the *hearse*.   —William Plymat

Pickled drivers cause more accidents than traffic jams.

When a man drinks to forget, he usually forgets when to stop.

O thou invisible spirit of wine, if thou hast no name to be known by, let us call thee devil!
—William Shakespeare, *Othello*

Christ and the liquor traffic have nothing in common. Christ came to redeem, uplift and ennoble the human personality. Liquor degrades and destroys it.   —*Telescope-Messenger*

Quick Quotes for Church Bulletins

Poverty never drives a man to drink unless he wants to go, but drink drives a man to poverty whether he wants to go or not.

You don't need alcohol for health; you don't need it for strength; you don't need it for food; you don't need it for drink; it never does any good; it always does harm. Let it alone.
—Bulletin of New York Health Department

In the "horse and buggy days" when a driver got drunk, there was enough "horse sense" left to get him home safely.

The business of the church is to get rid of evil, not to supervise it.

The chains of habit are generally too small to be felt until they are too strong to be broken.
—Samuel Johnson

Booze increases business—for the hospitals, ambulance drivers, doctors, nurses, undertakers, and grave-diggers.

Liquor fools the man who fools with it.

The liquor business is the mortal enemy of peace and order, the despoiler of men and the terror of women, the cloud that shadows the face of children, the demon that has dug more graves and sent more souls unsaved to judgment than all the pestilences that have wasted life since the plagues of Egypt, and all the wars since Joshua stood before Jericho.
—Henry Grady

King Alcohol prepares an empty table before me in the presence of my family; he anoints my head with hellishness, my cup of wrath runneth over. Surely, destruction and misery shall follow me all the days of my life; and I will dwell in the depths of perdition forever. —The Drunkard

Down on the farm. Alcohol will remove boards from the fence of the farmer, let cattle into his crops, kill his fruit trees, mortgage his farm and sow his field with wild oats and thistles. It will take the paint off his buildings, break the glass out of the windows, and clothe his family in rags.

Rum is all right in its place, and that is—in hell.

Alcohol costs a man not only dollars, but sense.

Whiskey! I never use it; I am more afraid of it than of Yankee bullets.
—Stonewall Jackson

One thing leads to another—drink, debt, dirt, degeneracy, devil.

Some of us think the little white ribbon (of the W. C. T. U.) is far more attractive than the big red nose.

To escape alcoholism is simple. Never take the drink just before the second one.

Parents who vote for legislation favoring the traffic in strong drink must not complain if their children fall into the trap their ballots help to set.

Statistics show that ten thousand people are killed by Demon Rum to every one killed by a mad dog. So what? We kill the mad dog and license Demon Rum. And we call ourselves enlightened and intelligent.

Most businesses like to exhibit their finished products. Not so the liquor interests. Look for their products in the gutter, down-and-out missions, and potter's field.

Does it make sense, for a few dollars to give one man the privilege of selling strong drink, then spend thousands of dollars convicting and punishing another man who commits a crime while under the influence of the stuff?

If all the officers united in setting the soldiers an example of total abstinence from intoxicating drinks, it would be equal to an addition of 50,000 men to the armies of the United States. —George B. McClellan

The tavern is a bank; you deposit:
Your money—and lose it.
Your time—and lose it.
Your character—and lose it.
Your health—and lose it.
Your manly independence—and lose it.
Your happy home—and lose it.
Your standing in the community—and lose it.
Your soul—and lose it.

When the liquor men are allowed to do as they wish, they are sure to debauch, not only the body social, but the body politic also.
—Theodore Roosevelt

I have better use for my brain than to poison it with alcohol. To put alcohol in the human brain is like putting sand in the bearings of an engine.
—Thomas A. Edison

From the point of view of health, there has never been any question but that abstinence from alcoholic liquor proves extremely beneficial.
—William J. Mayo

Leave drink alone absolutely. He who drinks is deliberately disqualifying himself for advancement. Personally, I refuse to take such risks. I do not drink.
—William Howard Taft

The United States reveres the memory of three martyred presidents—Lincoln, Garfield, and McKinley. It has been said that practically the last thing done by each of their assassins before committing their terrible deeds was to brace himself with strong drink.

A pint flask can cause a peck of trouble.

Horse sense is the ability to say "Neigh."

"One for the road" often means six for the hospital.
—National Safety Council

Drivers are safer when the roads are dry; roads are safer when the driver is dry.
—National Safety Council

Stay alive, don't drink and drive.

Just a drink or two, and a safe driver is turned into a reckless traffic menace. —Morris Fishbein

Alcohol Advertising—the Biggest Fraud in History
"I say what I am paid to say"
—In the theatre,
—On the radio and television,
—On the signboard,
—In the papers and magazines,
—In legislative halls.
"But, I tell the truth"
—In the wrecked automobile,
—In the laboratory,
—In the city jail,
—In the veins of the drunk,
—In wrecked homes and lives.

O God, that men should put an enemy in their mouths to steal away their brains! —Shakespeare

The ravages of drink are greater than those of war, pestilence and famine combined.
—William E. Gladstone

Alcohol is a mocker, a cheat, a liar, a bandit, a debaucher, a thief, a corrupter, a disturber, a murderer, a kidnaper, a ravager, a poisoner, a tyrant, a traitor, and a despoiler.
—National W. C. T. U.

A tavern can no more run without boys than a sawmill without logs. The question is: Whose boy? Yours, or mine?

I hate the liquor traffic, its greed and avarice, its corrupting influence in public affairs, for the cowards it makes of public men; . . . for the load it straps to labor's back; for the human wrecks it causes; for the almshouses it peoples; for the insanity it begets; for its countless graves in potters' fields; . . . for its moral degradation; for the homes it has destroyed; for the hearts it has broken.

I hate it as justice hates wrong; as liberty hates tyranny; as freedom hates oppression.—J. Frank Hanly

Believe me, no truer word was ever spoken than that the drinking nation is the carpenter of its own coffin and the digger of its own grave.
—J. A. Cullen

No man ever repented that he arose from the table sober, healthful, and with his wits about him.
—Jeremy Taylor

Booze builds business—for the undertaker.

The steady drinker soon becomes an unsteady drinker.

The man who drinks now and then usually drinks more now than then.

The drunkard in the gutter is in a better place for himself—and us—than behind a steering wheel.

Chapter X

Religious Life and Action

When you are facing the sun, your shadow will fall behind you.

The best command of language is often keeping still.

Men show their character in nothing more clearly than by what they think laughable. —Goethe

The lions did not devour Daniel because he was all "grit and backbone."

Drop a word of cheer and kindness;
   just a flash, and it is gone;
But there's half-a-hundred ripples
   circling on and on and on.
          —James W. Foley

Some Christians are puffed up about their own humility.

Loose dealing gets some into tight places.

One of the best ways to get on your feet is to first get on your knees.

You do not need more of God so much as that God needs more of you. He would possess you so that you may possess your possessions.
          —F. J. Miles

It has been said that "temperamental" means 95 per cent temper, and 5 per cent mental.

Do right or you'll be left.

There are no traffic jams on the straight and narrow way.

Why praise dead saints and persecute living ones?

Christians are the salt of the earth, and should be sugar, too.

Some people have strong will power, and some have strong won't power.

One of the devil's most successful wiles is, "Wait awhile."

Wit's end need not mean faith's end.

You cannot be a Christian without others knowing it.

Do not pray for rain if you're going to complain of mud.

You'll never go wrong doing right.
          —Norman Vincent Peale

A life of content is a life with content.

The way we are facing has a lot to do with our destination.

Smiling is a contagion for which we want no antidote.

Don't put things off—put them over.
—*Baptist Reminder*, Dallas, Texas

Many have quarrelled about religion who never practiced it.
          —Benjamin Franklin

Vice is a monster of so frightful mien,
As to be hated needs but to be seen;
Yet seen too oft, familiar with her face,
We first endure, then pity, then embrace.   —Alexander Pope

Are you looking for a soft place? Then look under your hat.

People usually get at odds with one another when they try to get even.

Making good use of a single talent can keep you pretty well occupied.

There would be less faultfinding if all the faultfinders had to come from the ranks of the faultless.

When a church stops doing, it starts dying.

This cold world needs warmhearted Christians.

Why look for your ship to come in if you have never sent one out?

Some people aim all right but they don't seem to know when to pull the trigger.

Excess often gets in the way of success.

It is the person who is afraid of being supplanted who ought to be supplanted.

Keep your shoulder to the wheel, and it is not likely your back will be to the wall.

The church cannot win its way in the world by following the ways of the world.

The true Christian is a person who is right side up in a world that is upside down.

Even the hypocrite admires righteousness. That is why he imitates it.

Learn how to live and you will have learned how to die.

The only way you can keep your religion is by giving it away.

A selfish Christian—that's a contradiction in terms.

It may be well to remind ourselves that we can't go the second mile until we have gone the first.

One "well done" by the Master is worth many encores by a human audience.

One trouble with a lot of people is that they are more interested in speed than in direction.

There are times when the gift of silence is as religious as the gift of tongues.

Great men never feel great; small men never feel small.

Some flatter themselves that they are atheists, when in reality they are only heathen.

Where will you be tomorrow? Are you sure?

Aim above morality. Be not simply good, be good for something.
—H. D. Thoreau

The "take-off" is very necessary, but it is continued flight that gets you there.

One thing you can do to make this a better world—you can improve upon yourself.

A religion easy to hide is easy to lose.

A lost temper needs no advertising.

Atheism is not an institution. It is a destitution.

Remember the week day, and keep it holy too.

Beware of the easy road. It always goes down.

Do not keep the alabaster boxes of your love and tenderness sealed up until your friends are dead! Fill their lives with sweetness! Speak approving, cheering words while their ears can hear them, and while their hearts can be thrilled by them.
—Henry Ward Beecher

It is wonderful how Paul covered so much ground and accomplished so much without a car.

A man is like a motor. There is something wrong with him when he knocks. The louder he knocks, the more serious his condition.

Your Own Version
You are writing a Gospel,
 A chapter each day,
By deeds that you do,
 By words that you say.

Men read what you write,
 Whether faithless or true;
Say, what is the Gospel
 According to You?
—Paul Gilbert

To pity distress is human; to relieve it is God-like.—Horace Mann

Man's extremity is God's opportunity.

The one thing certain about life here is that we must leave it.

When the outlook is dark, try the uplook. —Henry Drummond

There are one hundred and thirty-five passages in the New Testament where life is referred to, and only in seven of these is the reference to mere physical life. Life is an endowment in the body, but the reality of life is a thing of the mind, the heart, the will and the activities of the whole man. It becomes clear that life can only, therefore, be completely fulfilled and enjoyed in the spiritual capacities of character and service.
—J. H. C. Macaulay

The test of all Christian activity is, "Will it add to the glory of God?"

Fear God for his power;
Trust him for his wisdom;
Love him for his goodness;
Praise him for his greatness;
Believe him for his faithfulness;
Adore him for his holiness.

The greatest friend of Truth is Time; her greatest enemy is Prejudice; and her constant companion is Humility. —Colton

Certain thoughts are prayers. There are moments when, whatever be the attitude of the body, the soul is on its knees. —Victor Hugo

Unless you are a rabbit, we wouldn't advise you to put much faith in a rabbit's foot.

The greatest success is to be worthy of success.

A weakness of many of us is that we want others to be better than we are willing to be ourselves.

The true Christian life is life as it ought to be.

You can't change the nature of sin by giving it a high-sounding psychological, innocent-looking name.

Extraordinary work is usually done by ordinary people with extraordinary zeal.

Sin must be confessed or it will fester.

Man needs divine help most when he doesn't feel the need of it.

God works in and through and for people at the same time.

It is only the continuing Christian who will reach the continuing city.

Some people are more interested in what they descended from than in what they should be ascending to.

You're never going to get anywhere if you think you are already there.

Do *now* what thou wouldst do *then*.
—*Imitatio Christi*

None of us is responsible for all the things that happen to us, but we are responsible for the way we act when they do happen.

Better keep yourself clean and bright; you are the window through which you must see the world.
—George Bernard Shaw

QUICK QUOTES FOR CHURCH BULLETINS

The greatest homage we can pay to truth is to use it.
—Ralph Waldo Emerson

There is nothing that makes men rich and strong but that which they carry inside of them. Wealth is of the heart, not of the hand.—John Milton

Fame is a vapor, popularity an accident, riches take wings, those who cheer today will curse tomorrow; only one thing endures—character.
—Horace Greeley

Many of the so-called joy rides turn out minus the joy.

Yes, it would be wonderful if everybody behaved like he thinks the other fellow ought to behave.

The average person finds it easier to *bare* than *bear* the infirmities of the weak.

A slap on the back may not be good manners, but it's a lot better than a slap behind the back.

Rough paths often lead to desirable destinations.

Much trouble is caused by our yearnings getting ahead of our earnings.

One may have a low purpose in desiring a high place.

It is a fine thing to have your own way provided you have accepted God's way as your own.

For every man who has lost God because of a great sorrow, there are a thousand who have lost him because of great success.

Life becomes tragic to him who has plenty to live on but little to live for.

Every man must live with the man he makes of himself, and the better job he does in molding his character and improving his mind, the better company he will have.

When in Rome do as the Romans do, if the Romans do as they ought to do.

Do not be *driven* to prayer. Practice it as a normal, systematic privilege.

It is impossible to shirk any responsibility that rightfully belongs to us. We may deny that it is ours, may refuse the duty or the blame that attaches to it, but the responsibility we cannot escape.

If you wish your neighbors to see what God is like, let them see what he can make you like.
—Charles Kingsley

One thing many a person has yet to learn is that he cannot travel the wrong road and come to the right destination.

Nobody knows the age of the human race, but most of us agree it is old enough to know better.

Self-restraint is the flange that keeps character on the track.

Occasionally a man mistakes profanity for profundity.

Of what use is eternity to a man who does not know how to use half an hour? —Ralph Waldo Emerson

It's queer how we never get too old to learn some new way of being stupid.

I have had more trouble with myself than with any other person I know.
—D. L. Moody

Eventually secret sins make the headlines.

Soil erosion is something to worry about; also soul erosion.

If we claim God as our Father, we should act as God's children.

Do more for your religion and it will do more for you.

Now and then adversity is brought on by perversity.

One proof of a Christian spirit is to be able to disagree without being disagreeable.

A halfhearted Christian is just half a Christian.

The person who persists in courting trouble soon will find himself married to it.

Some who think they are on their way to heaven seem to be headed in another direction.

It is surprising how many know how to make a good living, yet do not know how to live good.

Kind words produce their own image in men's souls, and a beautiful image it is. They soothe and quiet and comfort the hearer. We have not yet begun to use kind words in such abundance as they ought to be used.
—Pascal

The only worth while security is courage; the only worth while power is love. Character and faith are the only things that count in the long run.
—Roger W. Babson

No one is useless in this world who lightens a burden for someone else.
—Charles Dickens

One can no more be mean and happy at the same time than an orange can at once be both sour and sweet.

You can tell what some men are by their bristles and squeal.

To be always exploding is no evidence of a dynamic personality.

We cannot be purer than our thoughts, higher than our ideals, nor greater than our dreams; therefore, we must think correctly, foster noble ideals, and rise on the wings of imagination to the highest things of truth and experience.
—*American Friend*

There can't be joy in salvation without sorrow for sin.

There are a lot of people who never forget a kind deed—if they did it.
—Adele Moore

Repentance is never too soon, it may be too late.

Love is a hammer that will break the hardest heart.

Too many petty causes get too much loyalty.

I find the great thing in this world is not so much where we stand, but in what direction we are moving.
—Oliver Wendell Holmes

To be utterly patient with men we need to think of God's patience with ourselves. —George Adam Smith

It should be a genuine comfort to know that God still has his hands on the steering wheel of the universe.

Isn't it strange how some people insist upon having expensive clothes, yet are satisfied with a shoddy religion?

Too many testimonies to the religion of Jesus are like testimonies to the merits of patent medicine—given by persons who never used it.

Some people must get sick before their religion is strong enough to assert itself.

There is a difference between defending your principles and defending your prejudices.

A lot of miserable sinners ought to feel more miserable than they do.

The grace of God knows no color line.

Some who boast of being hard-boiled are just half-baked.

Many are well prepared for a "rainy day" who are totally unprepared for eternity.

In the end, the things that really count are the things you can't count.

It is not good for a man to live alone—nor for a denomination.

There are too many semi-Christian Christians.

Seek ye the good things of the heart, and the rest will either be supplied or their loss will not be felt.
—Francis Bacon

Those who "throw themselves away" seldom like the place where they land.

Christ is needed on the avenue as much as in the alley.

What have you done today that nobody but a Christian would do?

The Golden Rule never tarnishes.

A good memory is considered quite an asset. There are times when it is well to have a good "forget-ery."

Laughter stirs up the blood, expands the chest, electrifies the nerves, clears away cobwebs from the brain, converts tears into the essence of merriment, and makes wrinkles expressive of frolic and youth.

If it doesn't affect your hands and feet, it isn't religion.

The best way to get your mind off yourself is to get it upon others.

The cash interpretation put upon the word "success" is our national disease.   —William James

There is something the world needs which only you can supply.

The longer I live the more I am convinced that the one thing worth living for and dying for is the privilege of making someone more happy and more useful. No man who ever does anything to lift his fellows ever makes a sacrifice.
—Booker T. Washington

Some still seem to think a merry-go-round life will get them somewhere.

A good vocabulary is no substitute for a good life.

Try understatement when repeating gossip.

A religion which produces no sunshine is all moonshine.
—Robert B. Pattison

Don't be so busy doing good that you have no time to be good—and vice versa.

Your strength is seen in what you stand for; your weakness in what you fall for.

Buy not silk while you owe for milk.
—C. H. Spurgeon

It isn't hard for some to practice what they preach, because they don't do much preaching.

When a man gets a "big head," it is an indication he has a small brain.

The man who expects to go to heaven should take the trouble to learn what route will get him there.

Sin causes the cup of joy to spring a leak.

Two people can't hate each other if both love God.

Jesus also is a very present help in preventing trouble.

The man who has an exalted opinion of himself is likely to be a poor judge of human nature.

In seeking happiness for others, you find it for yourself.

If you can't be a source of good, you can at least be a channel.

God hates sin, but loves the sinner.

A lot of churchmen ought to become Christians.

An artist makes himself an artist by painting, a musician makes himself a musician by playing, an athlete makes himself an athlete by running or rowing or wrestling, a merchant makes himself a merchant by buying

and selling, and so a professing Christian makes himself a real Christian by doing Christlike things.
—Charles E. Jefferson

You need not confess the sins of others.

The creed you really believe is spoken not by your lips, but by your life.

Too many of us are waiting for things that are not worth waiting for.

The greatest need of modern Christianity is the rediscovery of the Sermon on the Mount as the only practical way to live.
—E. Stanley Jones

If you did today all that you had planned, you didn't plan enough.

Sow an act, and you reap a tendency;
Sow a tendency, and you reap a habit;
Sow a habit, and you reap a character;
Sow a character, and you reap a destiny.

Many people want what they don't need, and need what they don't want.

There is so much good in the worst of us,
And so much bad in the best of us,
That it hardly behooves any of us
To speak ill of the rest of us.

The idea some seem to have of service is "serve-us."

You can't make hay out of wild oats.

Many who are quick to run into debt find it takes a long while to crawl out.

No one has permanent old-age security until he has provided for everlasting life.

Rugged individualism sometimes leads to ragged individualism.

Many live by the speedometer, rather than by the compass.

Life's bargain hunters usually wind up holding the bag.

He cannot hate man who loves God; nor can he who hates God love man.
—Chrysostom

"The wicked flee when no man pursueth." They make better time when someone is after them.

God never alters the robe of righteousness to fit the man, but the man to fit the robe.
—*Christian Union Herald*

There isn't any use trying to shine unless you take time to fill your lamp.

No man can hold another man in the gutter without remaining there himself. —Booker T. Washington

It's what you do when you have nothing to do that reveals what you are.

We also have conspicuous examples of self-unmade men.

What you are speaks so loudly I cannot hear what you say.
—Ralph Waldo Emerson

There is a difference between having to say something and having something to say.

I have tried to keep things in my hands and lost them all, but what I have given into God's hands I still possess.   —Martin Luther

God buries his workers but carries on his work.   —John Wesley

We cannot all have good fortune, but we can all deserve it.

The person who fears God has nothing else to fear.

One way to get ahead of your neighbors is by not trying to keep up with them.

People seldom get dizzy from doing good turns.

Quick Quotes for Church Bulletins

A genuine Christian is the best proof of the genuineness of Christianity.

Confessing your sins is no substitute for forsaking them.

Someone ought to invent an amplifier for the voice of conscience.

In this automotive age a lot of people are going everywhere without getting anywhere.

It is hardest to be accused of wrongdoing when the accusation happens to be true.

Take note that a lie is the beginning of liability.

It requires no musical talent to be always harping on something.

The more push one has, the less pull he needs.

The ships that come in while we sit and wait are mostly hardships.

Count that day lost whose low descending sun
Views from thy hand no worthy action done.

Profanity is the effort of a feeble mind to express itself forcefully.

Worry, like a rocking chair, will give you something to do, but it won't get you anywhere.

Many cannot enjoy the abundant life because of their abundance of things.

No, you don't have to make a trip to Paris in order to become a parasite.

Leaving Darwin out of it, there is a little too much monkey business in modern theology.

Playing fly for a spider must be great sport. Every sinner is doing it.

The four-square man is also well rounded.

Men are usually down on what they are not up to. —Hoyt M. Dobbs

Character is like a tree and reputation is like its shadow. The shadow is what we think of it; the tree is the real thing. —Abraham Lincoln

A gem cannot be polished without friction, nor man perfected without trials.

Life is not so short but that there is always time enough for courtesy. —Ralph Waldo Emerson

We have committed the Golden Rule to memory; let us now commit it to life. —Edwin Markham

Hardening of the heart ages people more quickly than hardening of the arteries. —Franklin Field

Quiet minds cannot be perplexed or frightened, but go in fortune or misfortune at their own private pace, like a clock during a thunderstorm. —Robert Louis Stevenson

Some men are hiding their light under a bushel, when a pint measure would serve just as well.

Religion consists of *credenda*, things to be believed, and *agenda*, things to be done. —Evan Daniel

There is no revenge so complete as forgiveness.

Be not disturbed by infidelity. Religion cannot pass away. The smoke of a little straw may hide the stars, but the stars are there and will reappear. —Thomas Carlyle

Wrestling with adversity may not be the most pleasant exercise, but it makes strong souls.

It is possible to be straight in creed, but crooked in character.

The greatest reward for Christian work well done is more to do.

A topsy-turvy world need not prevent one from keeping his own life right side up.

Don't expect to keep ahead if you permit yourself to lose your head.

We love ourselves in spite of our faults. Why should we not love others in spite of their faults?

By walking straight you are most likely to get into the best circles.

One test of bigness is doing little things in a big way.

There are no idle rumors. They are all busy.

One time when a fellow finds his credit good is when he sets out to borrow trouble.

If we cannot live so as to be happy, let us at least live so as to deserve it. —Fitche

Happiness in this world, when it comes, comes incidentally. Make it the object of pursuit, and it leads us a wild-goose chase, and is never attained. —Nathaniel Hawthorne

A man who has committed a mistake and doesn't correct it is committing another mistake. —Confucius

The more arguments you win, the fewer friends you will have.

It isn't necessary to put a marker at the grave when you bury the hatchet.

When everybody is saying the same thing, it is a sign that nobody is doing much thinking.

You may live a large life in a small place.

One should be made better by his religion or get a better religion.

It is well to know your own limitations; also your possibilities in Christ.

No one can claim to have a peaceable disposition merely because he is at peace with the devil.

People take your example far more seriously than they take your advice.

It is not unusual to find an open mouth and a closed mind in the same anatomy.

Say this for Rip Van Winkle, he finally woke up. Some never do.

In becoming a Christian you surrender only your liabilities.

Some people are going the second mile—in the wrong direction.

If you want to realize your own importance, put your finger into a bowl of water, take it out, and look at the hole. —Robert Burdette

"Sympathy costs nothing," is only a half-truth. Genuine sympathy always calls forth service that helps. The Samaritan's sympathy cost him a part of two days' time and some money, but it made him immortal as the world's greatest example of neighborly sympathy and helpfulness.
—*St. Louis Christian Advocate*

The Christian life is like an airplane; when you stop, you drop.

Make yourself an honest man, and then you may be sure there is one rascal less in the world.

The great tests of life reveal character; it is not until winter comes that we know the pine is an evergreen.
—On a Gravestone in England

God is Love. It is written
Throughout the universe,
Upon the cross of Calvary,
In the Holy Bible,
In the heart of every believer,
Upon everything the disciple touches,
In eternity.
—Author Unknown

Happiness adds and multiplies as we divide it with others.

Some people have the idea they are worth a lot of money just because they have a lot.

Superior people talk about ideas; average people talk about things; little people talk about other people.

What happens in us is more important than what happens to us.

It is only at trees bearing good fruit that stones are thrown.

It is better to swallow your pride than to eat your angry words.

The depth of one's convictions measures the breadth of his influence.

Act well your part; there all the honor lies. —Alexander Pope

The hottest places in hell are reserved for those who in a period of crisis, maintain their neutrality.
—Dante

Sometimes a man with a clear conscience is just one who has a poor memory.

You can't judge an auto by the sound of its horn—nor a man.

Keep your lamp trimmed and burning, and let God place it where he will.

What do we live for, if it is not to make life less difficult for others?
—George Eliot

Christianity is more than a belief or creed that saves one for the next world; it is a way of living. It is a life of love and service. The Christian is one who devotes his powers, abilities, and money to help others.
—D. C. Cook, Jr.

A little horse sense may prevent many auto accidents.

Your faith: use it, or lose it.

It is more important to know where you are going than to get there quickly. Do not mistake activity for achievement. —Mabel Newcomber

When a man imagines, even after years of striving, that he has attained perfection, his decline begins.
—Theodore Martin

Riches take wings, comforts vanish, hope withers away, but love stays with us. God is love. —Lew Wallace

Faith draws the poison from every grief; takes the sting from every loss; and quenches the fire of every pain; and only faith can do it.
—J. G. Holland

Sweet mercy is nobility's true badge.
—Shakespeare

You can't live wrong and die right.

We worship a God who is real;
We worship a God who is available;
We worship a God who is adequate.

Courtesy is contagious.

Religion is like a wheelbarrow—you have to push it.

Religion is like a bicycle—when it stops going, it falls over.

Let everyone sweep in front of his own door and the whole world will be clean. —Goethe

Keep your fears to yourself; share your courage with others.

Do unto others as you would have them do unto you, but do it first.

Friendship is a word, the very sight of which in print makes the heart warm. —A. Birrell

You can't keep trouble from coming, but you don't need to give it a chair to sit on.

Worry is interest paid on trouble before it is due.—William R. Inge

Profanity is an evidence of the lack of a vocabulary—and brains.

There is a difference between making a good living and living a good life.

I complained that I had no shoes—until I met a man who had no feet.
—Arabian Proverb

It is possible to be on the level and upright at the same time.

The world will be better either because you have lived in it, or because you have left it.

Some people lose faith in humanity because of what they see in the mirror.

If your religion leaves your life unchanged, you had better change your religion.

Dead is the religion which does not aim at these two things, personal purity and active charity.
—Thomas Guthrie

Too many rounds of pleasure weaken the ladder of success.

If wrinkles must be written upon our brows, let them not be written upon our hearts. The spirit should never grow old.—James A. Garfield

A man is not necessarily smart just because he says things that smart.

Set your mind on the eggs of discontent, and you'll hatch distress.

"It takes all kinds of people to make up a world." So runs the old saying. But we think we know several kinds we could get along without.

Let us endeavor so to live that when we come to die even the undertaker will be sorry. —Mark Twain

The hardest job that people have to do is to move religion from their throats to their muscles.
—Thurman Arnold

Be such a man, live such a life, that if every man were such as you and every life a life like yours, this earth would be a paradise.
—Phillips Brooks

Center all your thoughts on self, and you will have misery in abundance. —Charles Kingsley

The glory of religion lies in the reality of the good God.
—William Newton Clarke

The Church is God's workhouse, where His jewels are being polished for His palace. —Leighton

All that I have seen teaches me to trust the Creator for what I have not seen. —Ralph Waldo Emerson

The great essentials of life are something to do, something to love, something to hope for.
—Thomas Chalmers

One must be a live, wide-awake Christian before he can fall "asleep in Jesus."

Opportunity and ability add up to responsibility.

A sense of humor is the oil of life's engine. Without it the machinery creaks and groans. No lot is so hard, no aspect of things is so grim, but it relaxes with a hearty laugh.
—G. S. Merriam

All people make mistakes. That is why erasers are found on lead pencils.

We should not criticize a hog for being a hog—unless he is the kind that has but two legs.

When a man starts singing his own praises it is pretty sure to be a solo.
—Lake County, Indiana, *Times*

Be not angry that you cannot make others as you wish them to be, since you cannot make yourself as you wish to be. —Thomas a Kempis

To love our enemies is not easy, but it is Christian, and nothing less is.

Hot words come home to roost.

There is a wonderful, mystical law of nature that the three things we crave most in life—happiness, freedom, and peace of mind—are always attained by giving them to someone else.

Hail the small, sweet courtesies of life, for smooth do they make the road of it!   —Laurence Sterne

One ought to talk only as loudly as he lives—a rule which would deprive some people of the privilege of shouting.   —J. Wilbur Chapman

The purpose of the tests of life are to make, not break us.
—Maltbie D. Babcock

Not failure, but low aim, is crime.
—James Russell Lowell

To hear God speak once it were worth while to listen a whole lifetime.
—C. C. Woods

Instead of trying so hard, as some of us do, to be happy, as if that were the sole purpose of life, I would, if I were a boy again, try still harder to deserve happiness.
—James T. Fields

To be a Christian in a real sense is far more than wearing a label. It means living a life.

Man's extremity is God's opportunity. Extremities are a warrant for importunities. A man at his wit's end is not at his faith's end.
—Matthew Henry